Wakes on the Horizon
A Selection of Poems
Translated from Telugu

NS Murty

WAKES ON THE HORIZON

A Selection of Poems Translated from Telugu

NS MURTY

WAKES ON THE HORIZON
A Selection of Poems Translated from Telugu

NS Murty
002, Mytri Palace, 4th Main,
20th Cross, BTM Layout Phase 2, NS Palya, Bangalore-76.
Ph: 7760991795; nsmurty4350@gmail.com
Website: Anuvadalahari (teluguanuvaadaalu.wordpress.com)

Copyright © 2016 by NS Murty

Publisher
Vaakili
6003 Matisse Ln. Roanoke, VA 24018

For copies in USA
Vanguri Foundation of America, Inc
P.O Box 1948, Stafford, TX 77497
E-mail: vangurifoundation@gmail.com
Phone: 832 594 9054

Cover Page Art Work: **Anwar**
Cover Page Design: **Brahmam**
Book Designed at: **Akshara Creators**

Printed in the Uniter States of America

$ 15.95

Library of Congress Control Number: 2016912309

ISBN-10: 0-9977363-0-5
ISBN-13: 978-0-9977363-0-4

To
*My Parents
and
Siblings*

CONTENTS

7

8

Preface

Translation is a probation for original work... I hold. Even if one fails to produce original work later, no regrets; one had already been rewarded. The translator is twice blessed... first, when he reads the original, and second, when he reads while translating. The cathartic effect of the emotions is not only purgative, but also purifying and ennobling. It transcends the mundane to transport the spirit to the celestial.

I attempted some of the translations included here as a diversion from my disappointment for not having been able to continue my graduate study at University of Houston after Spring 2011 due to acute arthritis to both knees. I was not able to stand on my feet and was largely confined either to my bed or to my chair in front of my computer for over one year. Miracle as it may seem, more than the alternative medicine I took, poetry did help me come over my illness and I am now able to climb steps and back to my job.

Translation is a transmission of emotion from one language to another; from the poet to the reader. In proportion to the richness and ability of the transmitting medium, the language and the translator respectively, the transmission losses can be contained.

Poems have a human face and just as we have a temptation to make friendship with some people at first sight, I was enticed by these poems to translate them from Telugu. By consequence, I must add, this is not a representative poetry of my times or the trends. The selection of poets is very subjective in the sense, I have taken only those poems that are within my capability to translate. That's why, some of the best poems of many poets of this anthology you may not find here; many good poets have been left out for the very reason. At best, it is a pot-pourri of reflections on contemporary events in veiled expression; at worst, it is a fancy collection of translations of someone who identifies himself with the feelings of the poets here.

The poets presented here have fine sensibilities whether they speak about love, separation, memory, war, nature, human relations or their angst for the all-pervading rot in the society unsettling and disturbing the spirit within. The ease with which their fine sensibilities are expressed in as delicate a language as Telugu, I must admit, I am unable to translate into English because of the sad impoverishment of my linguistic resources. But, I can vouchsafe that the discerning reader will be able to perceive the moon behind the clouds of my imperfections ... since, Mind is closer to the Heart than Tongue.

I own responsibility for all the errors, omissions and inadequacies that you find in these translations. I sincerely thank all my poets for giving me permission to translate their works in the first place, and for acceding, now, to include them in this book.

I would like to put on record my deep appreciation and thanks to my friend and poet Ravi Verelly for making a nebulous idea of this book real in so short a time. I express my deep appreciation to my poet friend Elanaga for his quality addition to this book with his meticulous proof reading, artist of international repute Mr. Anwar for the art work and Mr. Bangaru Brahmam for the excellent cover design. I also express my thanks to Smt Sita Ponnapalli of Akshara Creators for her DTP work meeting all our demands with patience and Karshak Art Printers for producing this coveted book.

Bangalore   **NS Murty**
June 2016

VISWANATHA SATYANARAYANA

Your Chariot

Your chariot, O my Lord, is racing
With an ordained speed, uninterrupted.
This corp came under it, got crushed;
Blood streamed in pools and dried up.

That effulgent resplendent chariot divine
Had not stopped a wee, cognizing any snag;
Neither it made a turn around, nor divine
The instant roaring screams I let out.

The charioteer shall wash my blood stains
Off your carriage wheels tomorrow;
From the infinite sanguine stains pooled over there,
How to make out mine? Tell me, my Master!

❖

GURRAM JASHUA

The Burial Ground

Aeons passed; not one amongst this ill-fated dwellers
Had ever woken up. Pity! How long they sleep vegetable?
O poor me! How many moms were shattered and grieved!
Surely, these rocks were scald with the searing tears over years

Flourishes there on the new memorial sank in deep darkness
A lamp ... like fire-fly; But strange! It is not put out spite of
Running out of oil! Shall we call it a lamp? No. No. No. It is
The heart of that unknown, ill-fated mother had left behind.

Pens of poets, sweet sonorous gullets of songsters had
Rolled over this field, and shall. Have not the mortal remains
Of Kalidasa, Bharavi, and their ilk, reduced to motes
In Nature, unto earth, and from there over to potter's wheel!

❖

A Bouquet of Darkness

Blinked, and I got up, looked behind
Mate not to be seen nor heard, of any trace
My heart doubled up and throbbed
My gullet dried
And choked me up.

Called up, hailed up, and exhausted...
The tired heart broke all tangles in a trice...
I shot up into the sky
Even there
I found Overcast gloom.

With my shriek muted, vision blurred
Shutting out my wings in the dim
I dropped down to the earth
Even here
I witnessed 'newmoon'ian darkness

❖

Hymn of Hope

When nature slips into sleep steadily in your dainty delicate hands
Surrendering to the deep dumb darkness of the night at this hour,
my Lord!
Why do you push this frail, impaired Lyre at me bidding to set it and
sing?
I fear the string might snap, fail to tune or may not twang at all.

I can't play the Lyre like a black cuckoo, its sweet sonorous scores
Hiding amidst the thick mango foliage of the spring;
Pray leave me! Contrary, if you render the hymns suffuse with love
Pervading this universe, I will be too happy to subject my self to
them.

Should you insist that I sing anyway, the lyrics of love,
You having so passionately composed yourself and bestowed
upon me;
Sweeten this hushed, empty gullet of mine, charging it with your
glorious
Ambrosial Grace of compassion; I shall just lend my voice, and
render.

◆

DUVVOORI RAMI REDDY

The Cultivator

Tinkling of the ankle bells of graceful country women on their
way
To fetch drinking water from the pond, as sun's beaming rays course
thro'
The lush leafy labyrinths creeping up to the mounts of cots
At daybreak, sound sweet like the bubbly babbling of darling babies
Dangling along the roof curbs for a while sun's radiant beams,
Only which can dispel dense darkness, gold-coat your cozy cot,
Come! Wake up! Shed your sleep. It's time to herd cattle to heath.
They graze heartily, feast on fodder and the dew-clad blades of grass.

Pearls of sweat ski down her cheeks
Collect behind that smooth veil of hers,
And fight (as the veil flirts impishly with mammilla)
As Bangles jingle with each churn-of-curd
Don't you listen the sweet lays of your lady?

Is it mean to attend to one's own work? Can't you watch
Your woman running around exhaust attend menial chores?
Take that yoke and fetch lake water without demur, please her.
Believe me, such simple courtesies shall never ever go a waste.

Don't be a lazy laggard, or, while away your time with
Lackadaisical youth paying deaf ear to all wise says;
If farmers, who turn barren lands to green pastures with their sweat,
Turn idlers, who can save the people, feed them with fine food?

As the sweet nascent fragrance of the newly blossomed
                                    chrysanthemum wafts around
As wild flowers on the meadow blow up as if a jeweled carpet was
                                    laid in welcome
As the fields of rice that bow humbly with full crop seem a home
                                    for the Goddess Lakshmi
As the clouds of mist rolling in the sheen of dawn waft like a veil
                                    of cloth dashed in gold

So elegant looks, at the moment, the whole world
That it seems an oil on canvas, rendered
With his magical touch by the Heavenly hand,
Come, just have a peep, eastward.

◆

DEVULAPALLI

Her Eyes

In her eyes,
There are the dark delicate shades
Of the infinite expanse of the blue sky;
The still reflections in the pure crystal waters
Of a silent swelling lake are scattered here and there;
The susurrations at dusk of the settling darkness,
Lying amidst the umbrage in the crown of Cadamba,
Are heard now and then;
And on other occasions,
Tears rearing behind the black nimbi of the rainy season
Lurk behind them;
Though
They ring some sweet exceptional haunting chants in mind,
They are still,
Indecipherable rare romantic melodies...

❖

Translated from Telugu ● *NS Murty*   **21**

Ah!

Spitting fire
When I rocket up into the sky,
Wonder struck are...
They!

Spewing out blood
When I plummet to earth
Mercilessly... they
The very ... they!

◆

ARUDRA

Last Cry

Sir! Mr. Death Sir!
Pray mercy! I am many-childed.
True, I am in arrears of rent
From the very beginning to this rented-in life.

Sir! Mr. Death Sir!
Please paint the walls of desires white... for the festival
Youth's backyard wall is so dilapidated,
Kindly get it repaired, at least this year.
Let me assure you that I won't smear the walls
With mucks of sex. It's a promise!
From the eaves of dreary daily routine kitchen
Want drips...please take note of it.
Permit me to collect in vessels of sleep
The strain of contentment gliding down the awning of dreams.

Sir! Mr. Death Sir!
Please get the tiled-roof re-laid anew
Prices of ideals are sky-rocketing,
Sir! Kindly reduce the rent.
Pray, direct the other tenants
To put designs of altruism in front of their homes.
Kindly see that the well is deepened.
Alternatively, get it desilted.
You don't have to worry
I don't jump into it to commit suicide.

Translated from Telugu ● *NS Murty*   **23**

Don't fling the boxes of memories
And mattresses of experiences onto the street,

Sir! Sir! Sir!
We shall settle the accounts in the coming life,
Spare me for the present.

Sir! Mr. Death Sir!
Many-childed that I am, please be mercifully merciful!

◆

TILAK

Last Night

When God came to me last night
Looking wan and sat downcast by my bedside
Tell me, did I speak anything? Did I really say anything?
Did I mention to Him about the promising boy
So full of hope, who, after failing in everything,
Took away his life out of hunger?
Did I speak about the young damsel
Who dragged out her life selling her youth,
Got tired of it, and one fine evening committed suicide?
Did I unveil the heartbreak of the granny
Who jumped into the river
Hearing the news of her son's death in the war with China?
Did I brief Him about the agony of the peoples?
Or about the acrid smell of Time burning
In Congo, Cuba, Cyprus and Laos?
Tell me, tell me honestly
Did I ask Him anything about you, or me?
Or about the decadence of the world
Or did I compel, blame or accost Him
To speak about the venom
That filled the serene comely hearts.
I know I know where the weakest link lies in the chain
I know I know
That's why, when I saw the pitiful tears
Rolling down his cheeks

Translated from Telugu ● *NS Murty*   **25**

In the reflection of the lamp,
I got up suddenly seized with compassion,
Embraced Him, dried His tears, and consoled
And bade Him good bye,
Escorting him up to the turn of the street.
I know I know
When man turns out to be a Satan
Poor old man! What can He do?
After all, he is His own making.

❖

Poet Immortal

Taking a stroll for a while
On the shores of Time,
He returned
Throwing a pebble afar.
The puppy of world
Came wagging its tail
And looked at the pebble left
And tried to take a bite.
Never did it see
Such a piece of brawn before.
The stone the poet had left
Was teasing the puppy...
Like an eyeball pulled off its socket
It was looking in all directions
And even when it was not standing there
It seemed to puppy that it was watching only her.
The stone which took shape
Between earth and heaven
Escaped the nails of the probing sea
Rolling round and round
And burying itself like a seed
It shot green life up on death.

❖

Translated from Telugu ❖ *NS Murty*

VAZIR REHMAN

In the End

Nothing remains in the end!
Even the dreadful snake... that herald of death
Dissolves like a scrawl on water.
Some wild plant peeps out with passion
Breaking through the grave
Sapping the essence of the bod
Only to wither away soon.
Some small dirty cranial bone remains
Wallowing in sun and dust.
Rejected even by a hungry fox.
That's it! Nothing remains in the end!
Even that ethereal flower of youth
That morphed the captivating carnal expanse
Into an exuberant intoxicating music
Shall have to bite dust
With its hairline fracture on the bone.
The libertine must pack up and depart dejected
Leaving behind the ruins of body- temple
Abhorring the cold flaccid breasts
And the dead loathsome mocking memories
It's inviolable
For the red-tailed 'wicky-bird' feeding on oil
In the dead of night
To rise up suddenly into flames
And pass into nothingness.

That's all!
Nothing remains in the end!
Every morning is a teasing promise.
Every morning is a new seven-knot cessation.

Won't anything remain?
Not exactly.
In the end,
At different times, and in different forms
We remain in the cycle of birth and death.
We stand... nodding our heads
At the wonders of the Nature
Somewhere amidst flowers of grass
Or in the hollows of hills.
Or walking hurriedly in an ant line
We express our bewilderment
At the heinous acts of humankind.
We remain
In the end...
Eternally.

My Lord!

My Lord! The abode you commit me to live
Is an essence of intense darkness of the night;
A veritable trove of abject poverty, disconsolate,
And, dabbed in endless stream of tears.

And into that Stygian darkness my Lord! You once
Flourished, eons ago; and, that day my humble cot
Was pervaded with a passel of flowery perfumes
Wafted around by the winds of ecstasy!

That's all! Darkness took over the reign again.
This endless enduring darkness and I
Have been locked up in a bear-hug ever since
Reminiscing you, and your profile of that moment.

❖

Dilemmas at Dusk

One evening:

At Roxy Norma Shearer
At Broadway Kanchanamala
Which way to go is the problem
A student has confronted!

At Udupi Srikrishna Vilas:

Beckons to it Badam Halva
Salivating... Semya Idli
Choosing between the two has
Reduced to a puzzle to an employee!

The same evening:

Cascade of creditors this way
His Children's hunger that way...
"Whether to hang himself by noose
Or, should he plunge into an ocean"
To a familial man
The problem has truncated.

❖

Paradox

Man and Woman,
What a creation!
Complementing each other's pleasure
Like Cotton and Fire.

Man and Woman
What a creation!
For mutual annihilation
Like Cotton and Fire.

◆

A Poem That's Not a Poem

Slogans are not religion
There is no more welfare in morals
That the people in power parrot to people like you and me.
Damn them, they reck not their own reed.

Who do you think rejoice
When you and I die?
Only the politicians who incite us.
Corrupted that they are the old morals
They can no longer protect the current generation.

Oldies can't read
The contemporary cues.
If you and I were to write the 'History of Flowers',
There won't be spines or sabers; but
They won't allow us to write.
They don't let truth to spin or weave.
Truth is always antagonistic to the rulers' interests.

❖

Dualism

When you were here at my place,
I was there at your place;
When you were alighting at Madras
I was boarding a Calcutta-bound train;
You are the blooming aurora borealis of northern hemisphere
I am a pelican standing on the shores of southern hemisphere;
There is no love lost between us two,
It is capable of severing us further apart.

Your intentions and ideals are as delicate and beautiful as you.
You walked down gracefully over the cream of milk,
In the footsteps of the moon and over the lips of flowers;
I have no ideals; I have no faith in mere intentions
I am coarse and always look sullen;
I will be searching for truth over the barbs of life
And amidst puddles of slime.
Loving leisurely, and heaving heavy sighs,
You saunter with your playmates on the terrace;
I will be losing my hair unable to put up with
Primitive hunger and barbarous intercourse.
For you truth is real, meaningful and brilliant;
For me truth is frightening, meaningless and incomplete.
At what focus can we meet?
Or, on what latitude can we embrace?

O, you tremulous tendril of hibiscus
In a whiff of breeze at day break!
I am an owl sitting on the crowning branch
Of a Beech at dusk.
You walk towards the heavenly court
Spraying star-dust in your wakes
I shall squat here on the ash pile of my dreams
Counting my tears

❖

ISMAIL

Rembrandt

How to capture on the canvas
The golden hues that hop
On the cheeks, on the shoulders,
On the jewellery adorning a neck
And on the borders of silver-laced saris?
First, captivate darkness...
One that's very fat and robust;
Then, on its skin
Make indentures with knife.
Be merciless!
Through those indents
Tawny blood juts out
Only to coagulate
Under the cheeks,
Under shoulders,
Under the jewellery adorning a neck
And under the borders of silver-laced saris.

◆

The Blind Beggar

Whenever I travelled by train
I found him getting into it at some station
His daughter walking him, and following

He always rendered one poem or the other, taking
Only from the *Dasarathi Satakam*

And his voice remained the same-
Like one drowning in a well, in his former life,
Calling out for help and nobody within reach to listen.

That call echoed, ringing thin and died down
Struggling to stay alive in the gullet,
And at last, reached out to him in this life.
His eyes were those two sockets,
Which had yearningly looked around, then,
For help in hope, and stalled...
Life lay suspended in those eye slots
Till they found him, once more, in this life.

All through his singing; and
Whenever I looked at his eyes,
A feeling charged up in my heart
To rescue that drowning man from the well.
Meanwhile, stopping his song,
Begging for a coin here and a copper there, he would get down
After his daughter... and I was left there behind.

Dasarathi Satakam is a centum of poems with a refrain by the poet composer
Kancherla Gopanna (1620 - 1680), popular as Ramadasu.

Translated from Telugu ◈ *NS Murty*   **37**

ARUDRA

The Water-Clock

The train you await
Runs always a lifetime late.

Unable to wait for eons
You get into some damn train.
Your baggage of ideals
TTE books under "excess luggage"
You will be compelled to dump your trunks
Of yearnings in the break-van of dreams.

Before you could upload all your luggage
The train would start leaving the platform.
So, better you leave behind some of it
With your favorite heroes.

You shall never reach your destination in your lifetime.
Hence, resigning "Gee God! What have you done!"
Stay put, wherever you are!

◆

Evening Perfumes

She daubs
Evening perfumes
For my sake every eve.
The scent of thin shadows
Creeps under her chin and ears.
The aroma of a
Steady standing rain
Over a Casuarina plantation
On the sea-shore
Flares up in her tresses.
A whiff of the caves
The sun-lion sleeps at night
Sweeps over her body.
And in her eyes reflects
The essence of the blue sky
Where the stars twinkle one after another.

Flying down from everywhere
The crows
Set somber in the Tamarind

Then
From the very Tamarind
The moon
Would stretch his alabaster wing

❖

TILAK

Muse and Modernity

P_{al!}

Pal!
There is prospect for modernity when it imbibes poesy.
For that matter, poesy itself is modern.
But just for the touch of modernity and to say something new,
Why do you trouble yourself and torture me
With your borrowed-, ill-digested experiences,
Senseless imagery and haggard presentations
Warping words without purport and restraint
Trying to one-up Dylan Thomas in imitation?

To write
"In the wee hours of yesterday, I swallowed two knives
Poured Sulphuric acid on my tonsured head and chest,
Clipping my lips I stacked them on your back,
At this moment, my eyes are goldfish in potion"
Appears novel and glamorous.
But this is childishness plus madness multiplied by decadence.
This decoction backfires
This culture generates degeneracy.
Obscurity in poetry is permissible at times
But the reader should catch
The contours of your experience,
It must leave an indent,
And that darkness should be translucent.
And a poem should always open up
A fresh lease of first-hand experiences
That greet and grind the reader.

Each word is potent, each word is fine-edged,
Each detail has a meaning, a propriety.
Waggling pebbles in a can, don't dub it as great music,
Curse me not in ire, brother, I am not angry with you.
A harness makes no horse of an ass,
Donning Khadi makes no politician a Gandhian,
Modernity confers no acceptability to everything new,
Costumes can't turn a commoner into a king
A prosaic idea cannot be poetic by rhyme.
Poetry is an alchemy...the secret of which only a poet knows.
Kalidasa knew, Peddana@ knew
Krishna Sastry* knows, Sri Sri* knows.
Try to live in the present, reflect contemporary times,
Ventilate your house opening out all windows,
Welcome all currents in.
No matter what you say it must be yours
It must come out from within, tearing you open.
Don't resurrect the dead genres from the vaults of the past
Don't drive into the open
The crazy horses of ideas without tack and harness

Brother! Poetry must reveal the fulgent expanses lying within.
It must expand the bourns of creative consciousness
Whether it spits fire or sprays manna
Beauty and Joy are its ultimate aim.

@ *Allasani Peddana was the leading poet of the famous octet known as
  'Ashtadiggaja' in the court of Srikrishnadevaraya of Vijayanagara Empire.*
* *They were the contemporaries of the poet.*

❖

ISMAIL

Treescape in a Storm

It sways like a sea...
Why does this ungirdled garden grieve
Night and day in the ceaseless storm?
Curiously, why even the ocean imitates?
Maybe it rains perpetually in its heart.
Amidst such billowing turbulence
Why do birds retreat only to the tree-waves
That howl and hiss?

No sooner the easterly hurricane
Starts spinning its sinister snares, than the
Ships sail to the seas for refuge, they say;
As the trees flaunt to the wind
Their answer to its questioning of their roots
The erotemes of roots
Still hang in the vacuum left by the upturned.

And the graceful cities
Fattened by the questionables
Remain under the siege
Of surrounding sheets of brimming brine.

Hands may cede, but,
Seeds and birds shall take wings.
Casting new shadows
Humming new hymns.

For the storm and the swelling surfs
They say,
Agitation is only at the periphery...
But at heart
They are both pacific.

The Rain

Like a childhood friend
Seen after long years of separation...
A drizzle
Raining delicately
Like a shower of jasmine petals
Embraced me with all its hands

Unable to realize a wee-bit
How good a friend he was
People ran for cover towards dry shelters
To protect their heads from getting wet

Just me and the rain!
Nobody else was there on the roads.
Since it was an uninterrupted togetherness
We roamed the whole town
Resting hands on each other's shoulders

In the nets of the drizzle, we filtered
The fish of our childhood stories
Catching and leaving them alternatingly
And were bone-tired loitering
Steeped in the rain of friendship

Coming on a seasonal tour
And spending this whole day with me
Rain bade me good-bye.

Though the clouds that brought him here had vanished,
Like the brilliant smile he left behind
A Rainbow stuck to the sky
Like the soaked shirt sticking to my skin.

❖

Everything That is Active

Somehow
I like more...

The sky
That endlessly stretches its hands
In all directions...

The waters
Whether they overwhelm the banks
Or attenuate to a bare ten-foot tributary
But, nevertheless run...

The wheel on the move
Even if it were
That of a child's tricycle...

The nib of a writing pen...

The mote of dust wafted by the wind...

And, even the wall-clock
That runs half an hour behind...

Than
A beatless heart
Like yours.

◆

SIVA REDDY

Akunta! Akunta!*

What to speak of her!
She can kick the globe like a balloon,
Can roll up the sky and
Tuck it under her arm,
She can go on flight with the birds
Flying atop the Neem tree
And can land on the floor like a butterfly,
Else, she can sit delicately on the flowers.
What to speak of her!
She is a sorceress!
She can do everything in no time
And can wail without doing anything.
Imagining is her forte!
She can bind people bound to part
Can breathe life into a terminally ill.
Arresting all spectral colours in her fist
Can spew them on our faces in disgust
She is quick to repeat whatever you say,
Meaning doesn't matter
Playfulness is her motto!
The title of the poem she now spins... is
Akunta! Akunta!

Note: Akunta, Akunta is a childy expression for I'd play I'd play.

◈

Translated from Telugu ◈ NS Murty   **47**

An Exposition of Peace

The peace we long for
Swings between
The point of a bayonet and the heart beat
Like a dying man's last breath
The peace we long for
Lies on the bed.

The peace we long for is a temple, a masjid,
An explosion, a cease-fire, an ending, a continuance
An injured song, a thunder of lightning
Dropped, snapped from heavens.
It's like the foot of a banned poem
Buried in the gullet.
Amidst the sonorous expositions of peace
By the bearded Mullahs and Sadhus
The peace we long for gasps for breath.

The peace we long for
Is lame like the gait
Of a dog that broke his leg.

Pity!
We have to get on
With whatever amount of peace
The state rations us
Collecting it in our bags.

A Black Love Poem

1

Will you agree at least now
That there is no invisible love?

2

All that remained between us
Were some apprehensions
And few insults still.
And after that
Either you shoot me
Or I shoot you.

3

No.
Faces of people
Are not just colorful flora
Or green foliage;
Neither woods, nor skies
Nor clouds nor mountains.
They are colours...
And at this moment
They are either white or black!

4

Can't you declare, even now
That all our love and laughter
Was a mere masquerade?
That it is only veritable hatred?

Translated from Telugu ● NS Murty   **49**

5

After so many pages of history
And after several emotional journeys together
You remain ultimately one color
And I ... another.
That's all!

6

Wasn't it just mistrust
That sufficed to chase and pull the trigger?
One look, just one look
To throw out your body
The life within
And the beats of its lively heart
Like a rot soiled quilt!

7

Will you admit
At least now,
Our love is dichromatic?

◆

ADURI SATYAVATHI DEVI

A Colossus

Whenever he runs into me
The stink envelopes me even before.
Embalming his skin with earth
He enters like clay sundered by the wintry wind
With a basket of dung over head.
He infuses life into the awaiting plants
Combing and caressing the roots.
Greeting with his looks
He teaches words to the sprouting twigs in silence.
Doctoring the infested and the diseased
He bathes the Banana saplings
Like new born babies
Standing them in order of school children.
Taking the charity of his labour
And relishing the music of his crooning
The tap roots transform to milky-ways.

Been sunburnt the whole day,
Sweat and soil disconcerting,
He asks for water becoming a bowl of thirst.
Bringing it in a dazzling steel vessel, I demur.
Reading the essence of my hesitation
He drinks his thirst out cupping his hands
And throws at me a smiling glance.
I sink my head to that look
Which bears the aeonean nobility and forgiveness.

He walks away...
Like a colossus
Straight and upright.

◆

K GEETA

A Lesson

Always
World is something - dreaming is another.
Living is something - life is another.
When we just blossom and about to turn a leaf
We think we can undo and rewrite the past.
Come what may, we think we can stand up to things.
Translate 'night-sheet'ful of dreams into day.
Wearing verdurous vivacity on our collars
We celebrate the world was created for us.
Suddenly, we realize the truth
Like a severed branch smashing over head
Time, along with the earth, begins spinning around.
It becomes imperative to sprout again, standing where you are...
Exigent to well up the snapped hot-water springs within.
You don't find a helping hand unto death, from terra to firmament.
You find either a sea or a desert around up to the horizon.
You shall have to fear for many things you never did;
Digest many things you could never stomach;
Run after the dreams spite of being sensible to reality;
Have to march ahead levelling the time heaped about.

Always
'I' is something - 'We' is another.
Women are something - and men are another.

❖

Translated from Telugu ● *NS Murty*   **53**

KONDEPUDI NIRMALA

Hope Against Hope

She abhors moonshine.
And detests the drizzle.
She vents impatience
At the inability of her dwarfish hands
To reach out to Rajahmundry from Bezawada
And her vengeance over the world and
Something she can't name or express
While locking the door.

Scurrying out with a lunch box stuffed in hurry,
Hanging on to the bus, to the rickshaw, to her own walk,
And to the nail-biting typewriter,
Dragging the day with black carbons till night fall
With bought out sleep and endless dreaming,
And even in those fortuitous fortnightly love-plays
She remembers only swearing of the boss for asking for leave;

Before they could rehearse how to open up
With the none-too-assuring words,
The devil of a train blares the whistle
And they withdraw their embracing looks.
"I remain, ta-ta, take care of your health,"
Become routine hackneyed phraseology.

For the miracle of getting tethered to the same post
They go on sending application after application
Reassuring their existence through

Postal-delayed letters and
Connected and disconnected calls,
With the fond hope... that, at least,
"Passed away" message
Reaches the other partner on time.

❖

SOWBHAGYA

A Dab of Music

I am a lake...
You are a gentle ripple
Bringing a dream along with it
Which rollicks on its surface.
In a still stony silence,
I await you without batting an eyelid.
Pray, come! Bringing along a mild breeze
That gently shakes your meandering tresses...
Humming exotic, ecstatic tunes.
I pray! I pray!
Toss that flowing hair over me
And let me watch you as I would a starry sky.
Strange but true, I feel lighter
Whenever you enter into my thoughts.
Those swaying leaves
And the butterflies that deftly wheeze past them
Feel as light and waft with me.
I glow whenever you shine in my thoughts
And my surrounds spring back to life.
Pray, come!
Like the Jasmine which anoints music
Dozing with invisible scents,
And like that Rose
Which empties all its grace into its full-blown petals,
I pray!
Comfort this un-smelt heart
Soothing with your breath of assurance.

❖

NIRMALA GHANTASALA

The Other-end of Life

Know not where we have come from.
Nor how the lustrous drive... stretching endlessly
Tapers off to a trail of luminescence
And gets engulfed in the endless sooty sea.
Aren't those pubescent countenances
Beauteous black mascara streaks among us true, or, only myth?
Should these wits and shades of moon wilt under funeral band?
Does cradle of Death for eons rock to put man to eternal sleep?
Does damsel Death continue to steal
The lukewarm human heaving stretching her icy hand?
For that matter, if one of us were to leave suddenly
What would happen to these enthralling tunes,
Oceans of excitement, shake hands,
The sensuous cheeks that pulse to the caressing strum of a rail,
Lukewarm emotions, blazing noons, nano-noted nights?
Who knows what?
Does moon then still yearn for us?
At least, will an eye get wet in grief?
Does the dank darkness deliver a shimmering jewel like us?
Who knows! Who knows!
Having thrown the die-hard death amidst so many 'who knows's
Arriving coolly as a guest at the most unexpected hour
Does she bite the knot of breath, in a breath?
Like a staggering slate-pencil,
Doesn't she squiggle the death-sentence?
Is it inevitable that the sudden silence should abruptly scissor

Translated from Telugu ◈ *NS Murty*   **57**

The world we so immensely love,
And the capering activity around?
And walk over us?
Must the corporeal cease? Should laughter be so short-lived?
Is departure the terminal truth?

I know that the other end is all darkness.
Pushed out of this body,
I would be an ethereal, colorless, shapeless disjoint chain.
The truth ...that once life gets separated,
With the haplessness of lacking shape, taste or voice
I would remain watching the hiccoughs wailing over me...
Is the worm that eats into the pleasant fruit of the 'present'.

◆

War and Enemy

We crossed the seas,
We crossed the deserts,
Crossed forests and firmaments.
Now, we must cross ... the wars.
Swim across the impending calamity
Of war spreading before man.

There is but one world
And only one man.
It's the existence of the earth
That confers all creation
A state of being.
It is the man alone
Who glows with life,
Like a lamp
On the pinnacle of the world.
But it is war
That prevents the world from being the world.
And it is the very war
That throws man off into the abysses
From every summit he conquered.
War
Is the fever that the world is afflicted with.

The enemy who trespasses boundaries
Also trespasses the no man's land

Between civility and barbarism.
Then, one has to win
Not only the enemy but also the war.
Like all people of a country
Combine to fight their enemy,
People world over should unite
To win over the war now.
They must isolate war along with the enemy.
Like reaching a plateau crossing the forest,
Like entering a garden passing the burial ground
We must enter peace crossing the war.
Enemy is an abbreviation of war
Win over the enemy
Conquer the war.
Once there is war, both parties lose.
The only war that both parties win
Is the war that was never fought.

We viewed skies unspanned by vultures
Observed lakes uninfested with crocodiles
Watched rains showering no thunderbolts.
It remains, to see a world without war.

◆

When the Vowel in Me is Lost

After a lifetime,
Dear daddy!
I get to know you… gradually
And ever slowly.
Like a warm sigh died down…
Like the dim blinking evening lamp in the niche
Refusing to blow out or snuff out.

The lesson of life...
What hundreds of dawns
And few more hundreds of evenings
And the silent nights and friendless midnights
And the un-thawing gloomy days
Had failed to teach...
Turns a new leaf today.

After you had completely slipped down my eyes,
This house became a boat afloat
On the river of infinite silence
Following your absence.
Only after you had left,
In the shadow of the lamp lit near your head,
Perhaps, I was really noticing you.

I am a hovel
Leaning on the post of a deep sigh
Perplexed as what to choose
Between life and death.

Translated from Telugu ● NS Murty   **61**

Death is an untaught lesson ... every time.
The same monotonous repetition,
Of a fly
And a peacock's feather,
On the same page.

◆

Currency Sword

These are times of liberalization war.
Days when the world dances
Before the drawn hood of a coin.
No matter whosesoever mind's silent vale you enter
It smells rat!
Through the whole stretch from snow to sea
Fluttering on the pillar of money
You hear the roar of a yawning rupee-lion.
No other animal-bob
Possessed this dexterity of archery
As the money-bob
That swings between the lips.

All countries might be anthills
But are homes to money serpents.
It's a damn lie that ants eat out serpents
It's a veritable truth that
Snakes strike at ants.
Nobody knows when one country's money snake
Enters the territory of another,
But one can hear the jingle of currency torsos
In the ever growing dreamy mindscapes.

There is destruction not only in the hot porno scenes,
You will witness destruction every day.
On the kaleidoscopic silver screen,
In the waltzing limbs of rupee,

In the vaulted money spinners, and
In the secretive market menagerie.

Nobody bothers who revolts against whose violence
Or assaults with rupee knife.
All that matters is
How not you question its deceit
How not you destroy its destruction.

That is why
You are not concerned of
A granny under the weight of a coin
A sweet darling great-grandchild,
A women being burnt alive on the streets
Or the untouchables...broiling in war.
In the field of failed matrimonies,
And melting of love-birds
Taj Mahal had long lost its relevance.

Today,
The relation between man and man
Has reduced to what a coin holds with the other.
Even while you take a wink
The currency sword chases you.
When the whole world comes
Under the spell of a coin
What to speak of a simple man
When the spiraling prices of pulses
Land their legendary 'third foot'* on his head,
Or the oil prices burning on the coals of market,
Or the ghosts of shares
That swallow town after town!

Soaring prices
Can always make a war-cry but never a war.
They can't even change a subsidized rupee,

Let alone a liberalized rupee.
Now man is no longer
A mass of flesh and blood that walks erect:
He is a round rupee coin
That relentlessly rolls down the slope

*Legend goes that Vamana, the fifth incarnation of Lord Vishnu, beneficiary of three
feet of land from Sovereign Bali, occupies the upper and nether worlds of the universe
with his two feet, and when there was no space left for his third foot, Bali offers his head in
culmination of his promise.*

❖

ADURI SATYAVATHI DEVI

The Epical Touch

To mine eyes long forgotten dreaming
And to my heart's precincts shut for ages
There came an eyeful ocular epic
Handing me out an invitation
And churned a new lyric in me.

The blue herds leisuring out on the sky
Must have hugged dearly the yonder hills
For, they drench in the cascade
Of warping blue hues.

Carrying fragrances,
Fresh blooms in the floral palanquin
Wind throws a song
Among a plethora of chirrupy chips.
And lo!
In a while the whole vale wells up in symphony,
Gay capricious youth is at play.
Over the tree trunks
Notched up by the wintry wind
Mischievous shoots peep in.

A verdure velvet carpet
Spreads evenly across the forest.
The blushing Kasiratnams gleam over it.
Grass flowers and tender Parijata enchant butterflies.
The unity of divergent beauty

Seems an 'Eye-ken' blessed by nature.
To unveil these charms
Lazying in wafer dew blanket
The sire, above the oriental line
Comes with chilled hands of delight
Comely cuddling and delicately embracing each heart.

That dawn of warm sunshine
Is a wreath of blossoming ideas.
There
Where unity alone abounds,
Is a message of peace;
The purity of a new born baby.

From the magma of my experiences
From the shades of arresting landscapes
From the elevated souls of ancient seers
Here comes a new man... walking down
The farmer... who can cultivate peace upon earth.

❖

Fragrant Soil

It is a surprise
If man is ignorant of
The fragrance of the soil,
Which he is born out of
And unto which he ultimately returns to.

Whenever it rains
The scent of nascent vapors of earth
And the aroma of the
Delicate natal baby blossoms
On the young green plants
Shooting from the earth
Pervades all around;

The bond with the soil
Is an enduring bond
And a true elemental sensory tie.

Is there a treasure richer than the toil?
And a perfume sweeter than sweat?
For the slogging hard-laborers
Sweat is their scent
Tear is their tincture
And soil is their substance.

Earth is a means for life
And a Mother of all resources.

Any man who serves this earth
Is my god supreme!
And the smell of that soil
Is an attar for me.

K GEETA

The Last Touch

My last respects to the feet visible on the funeral bed
This touch is the last memory of daddy for all his life.

*

Daddy! Daddy!!
Did your sins agonize?
Or your tell-tale hand on mother's neck torment you as wounds?

Ineluctable throes
Before heart rests or life ceases!
How touching was your wailing unable to endure,
Substituting the voice failed three years thence with your fingers!

Whenever tears well up for you…
Your keeping me guard dozing outside the rest room,
Boxing my back when I did not heed your word,
My sister and I playing merry-go-round with your hands, and
The cracking of our bones
As you removed the body-pack, once a year, for Pongal…
Are the few, little, hazy memories that flash in my memory-scape.

Whenever mother's eyes filled with tears
I felt like burning you with petrol
But strangely, yesterday, I wished you were rather alive.
Forsaking your duties, living only for yourself
What did you achieve?
Extreme pleasure and extreme grief!

You became a specimen for people how not to be,
And couldn't be a coveted figure in any heart.
Didn't I tell you that you will be relieved
And everything would be alright?
Being aware that death is the only cure for you,
I told you to buck up and not to worry.
How can I forget and when can I forget
Those eyelids eagerly searching for me in the last hour?
With pangs entreating me to hold your hand?

You were a devil that put my mother to every hardship.
You were a father who no one would ever like,
But yet, I felt a part of me had burnt to ashes.
When brother called 'Daddy!' into your corporal ear
I had an urge to shake you up and take you back home.
As the filing logs concealed your hands and bosom
I felt like crying you can't bear that burden.
When I witnessed your skull incinerated in the raging pyre,
The grief piled up to heart's brim, had ultimately burst out.

❖

She and Her Room

Whenever I sit in her room
The blue-shifts of her starry exhales
Reach, glowing unto me, from her eyes.
Like a Mediterranean island
Basking in moonlight
She sits alone amidst four walls
And me, alone with her.
Making me a scorching sentence
She takes me along hugging, as she does a pet deer,
Into unhurt corporal locales.
The room
The translucent air within
And her glistening moist looks
Make me an innocent convict awaiting sentence.
Eons of dreams melt like candle wax
Through the rustle of calendars
And the overwhelming urge
Wanes in the strings of sound silence...
Whenever I carry me,
The yet unknown me to myself, to her room
Strange worlds embrace my knees
And two lives explore secret after secret.

SATISH CHANDAR

A Birth Deferred

My heir always puts me the same question:
"Father! When do you expect me?"
I stand before the full length mirror.
Not a six-pack body
But six-lakh insults shall I see therein.

Whenever I look at my close crop of curls
Recalling the knotted hairs of my grandfather
Who was denied both scissors and razor,
I comb it smooth with vengeance.

When the two ears like lamp posts
Are all ears for the blazing music,
I feel guilty within and draw the cropping
Over eardrums as cover lest some
Liquid lead should be poured into them.

When the tightly drawn lips
Ventured to assay a smile
I recall the cups of venom my forefathers traded
For their heartache from charming high-caste women
And I flood my own reflection with kisses.

When I button my full-hands shirt
I recall my mother walking to the village outskirts
With nothing but an airy-raiment over her bosom
And my hands inadvertently feel my shoulders alternately.

As I tighten the sleek belt around my girdle
I sense the hustle of an ethereal presence behind
Trying to erase my history with my own hands
And search perplexed all around for clues.

When I tighten the lace on the sparkling shoes
I feel I had listened to the moans of the bleeding feet
Of my father that only mother earth had kissed,
And I bow in reverence before I stand.

And lastly, when I attempt a curlicue with my moustache
Before walking out, I recall the officer's disparaging remarks
"Oh! The 'reservation'ist flaunts his manliness! Huh!"
And swallow hard the past-present tense.

Then my heir asks me the same question:
"Father! When do you expect me?"
Walking aside the full-length mirror
I beat endlessly on the old drum
Of my grandfather's hanging on to the wall.
The sound aborts, and a birth gets deferred.

❖

MUKUNDA RAMA RAO

A Smile on Migration

When my own bustling beaut blossom
Bids me good-bye
It seems as though the dove
That huddled close to my heart this long
Has taken wing
Throwing a misty screen fore eyes
Knowing fully well
Like a Siberian bird on migration.

That she has packed up all festivities and frolic with her
So soon, makes us think we don't exist amidst people.
It is not until one comes tête-à-tête with it
No pang or pain would ever be understood

Those capering leaps
Childhood sand dunes and
Captivating mischief, adorning the house still,
Reminds everybody of her.
There are no wakes of her taking off
Except the agony of not finding her here.

Even you and I won't leave out
All plants that shoot up ... at one place
Nor leave all fruits to the branches that bore them.
The paroxysm of partition
Does not touch the hands that part.
Else, notice the hand

Not sure if it be a sure hand or not
Like the pride of the victorious over the vanquished,
Holding her hand, he sports a glittering smile
Exactly like me... sometime during the past.

◆

The Seedless

The seed
Has become unviable.

1

You and I
Are now a desert each
A Thar... A Sahara...

2

The path lays there like a tired breath
Our path ... in that wild.
The course smothered under our steps
Is like a lone cob glistening through your mantle...
It is a smile dashed against the shores of my lips...

3

That land is no more,
With fields bowing under heavy harvest
And our hands grazing over them.
There is no more that scaffolding
Nor the dreams we once dreamt lying there.

4

There's no river
Nor our feet dunked in it
Neither the ripples they created there
Nor the fish that kissed them.

5

No,
There is not a drop in the river
Nor in our eye that anxiously follows it.

6

Is this reticence?!

KAVI YAKOOB

The Run Within

Did I properly lock the door?
Did I switch off the geyser?
Did I keep the milk bowl back in the frig?
Oh, damn it!
The three kittens might make a hell by the time I come home.
Well, maybe the tommy might not allow barking at them
And might chase them away towards the gate.
But sometimes it sleeps like a log.
Btw did I logout from the laptop
Did I leave the FB open as it is?

Oh, bloody traffic and bloody traffic signals!
Caught in the jam as usual and resent it as usual.
A vacuous feeling if I don't resent.
There is only twelve minutes left for office.
Can I reach office in time? Can I sign in on time?
Awful signal! How long shall I have to vent my anger
On these traffic signals?

Poetic diction has changed; metaphors have changed.
In the confused and confounded life...
The scars of wounds from the run within lay scattered around.
There are traces of my blood
In the flood swelling breeching the roads.
Like the teething pain of stiff joints...

There are no dialogues between people.
Neither conversations anymore.

All talk turns out to be a ranting of credits and debits.
A life that exists between two pay packets at a time...
And reduces to a veritable P&L Statement
With its bills payable, liabilities, and net losses.

Occasionally, some books and few people
Like paintings on heart's canvas
Lend their color to our lives.

The dream of Sunday recurs for the rest of the week.

A life... Sans traffic, sans locks, sans run...
A blank dreamless dream

◆

ADURI SATYAVATHI DEVI

The Bay at Bhimili

When I walk about that way
Spread-eagling my curious looks
I get a feeling of sneaking through a new window.

Lapping itself up in several folds
The Sea seems a primordial man
Swathing under its watery covers.
Like somebody tickling you to wake up
When the sun was high on the sky
The Sea moves languorously
Spraying smiles of surf all around.

Sprinting up to beach sands, terrain,
And swaying with its frothy bubbles,
Like the anklet bells of a baby,
It appears a silken cloudlet aground.
With its eons-old eagerly looks
It dreamily awaits the first baby-boats
Tossing over its chest.

How many juvenile infatuations it must be hiding!
How many sweet nascent ideas it must have swallowed!
Leaping tide over tide
It presents itself in consummate beauty.
For the incoherent babble of the wind in my ears
My heart aches--- with a spring of poetic urge.

Translated from Telugu ⬧ NS Murty   **81**

But, before I could make any headway,
The string of inexplicable ideas vanishes into ether.
That's why I feel
One could only preserve those luscious sceneries in mind's eye
Than could ever fix them in poetic diction.

❖

A Railway Station

When the train arrives on a platform
I look at the station through the glass window
And pick up each image:
A boy on his mother's breast,
A foreign lady with a rucksack hanging on her back,
A destitute boy
Carelessly booting everything in his walk,
Two playful puppies in the distance,
And under the trees, people sitting
As if they had been sculpted on stone,
A woman fleeing wailing, and following her behind
A man, husband or somebody, throwing vulgar abuses at her
As if he had a right to abuse her... and she,
As if she had a right to run away from him.

When the train halts
I watch the scenes changing one after the other...
Like gleaning the coins scattered from the floor...
Like combing a disheveled hair.

Friend who promises to meet me at the station
Comes only after train starts leaving
And standing on the other platform
Waves his hands towards me making gestures...
Eyes meet... but words do not reach each other.
Perhaps looks are also a kind of conversation
Sharing it fifty - fifty

Translated from Telugu ● *NS Murty*   **83**

He... standing steadily there
And I... moving away like this...

Nothing remains static.
Nor anything remains for that matter.
The station opening out its mouth
Swallows me and my train.

KONDEPUDI NIRMALA

Chilling Stories

I am scared
Of the word motherhood.
The constant fear that I might not be able
To discharge my motherly obligations
Unnerves and defeats me.

My children eulogizing me
As motherhood incarnate
In lyrical panegyrics deludes me
As kids' vomiting's, viral fevers, soiled laundry,
And the milk bottles and nipples left for boiling
Confirm my square responsibility,
And my loneliness amidst a teeming family.
The scornful neglect and indifference
Meted out to mothers in their sunset years
Bankrupts my faith.

Why do you bother me?
If you want to lick a few beautiful lines about mother,
Or, somehow want to scale the slippery ridges
To reach the starry heights overhead
The agony behind that motherhood
Is beyond the ken of your marketing mind-set.
For,

I have no choice to my pregnancy;
I am compelled to know the sex of the foetus,

Translated from Telugu ◉ NS Murty

85

And
I can't even choose the numbers of my hellish labor!

The more you comfortably hide yourself
In the gross chilling tales with worn-out laughs
Sweating blood and shedding warm tears,
The more you get inspiration
To churn out nobler and exotic lyrics.
If there is a Nobel for awarding to mothers
Better present it to your fathers instead
For deftly handling their urge to sire and sex
To make merry of our basic feminal rights.
But, please
Never make poetry a ready handkerchief
To blow your nose as casually as you did
With our sari frills when you were children.

◆

K GODAVARI SARMA

A Double-edged Sword

In the bubbling enthusiasm of my youth
I used to snarl at the oldies
For coloring their passiveness
As mellowness and maturity

After getting worldly wise
I call the youth uncouth
For their delusion of
Mellowness and maturity
As passivity

The Last Journey

Is the distance between life and death just a step?
Oh, lady! You who logged all these distances in steps,
How could you fail to put that single step forward?
How did that six-inch rail, tell me,
Had suddenly become a six-foot wall?
How do you know?
Who gave you the role of a scare crow?
Or, who authored this Beebhatsa Rasa?
Whether you had walked, crawled or rolled all your life,
But your last journey was performed at sixty mph.
Who would answer if one questions
Their right to drive trains at speeds
They haven't yet learnt to bring them to halt instantly?

Travel he might at whatever speed
And however long...
Can man produce one, just one, life-particle?
The fingers that built many great cities,
Skyscrapers,
Machines, airplanes and trains
Can create a little finger again?
Is it necessary to reassert that the man
Who can see, walk, think, and talk
Is a great wonder?
Man may come out of man
Like the Doll Family of Etikoppaka

One from the other for generations...
But who can create a man out of raw materials?

Who can explain what life is?
Who can give life?

Moon may now be a ball of butter in the palm to man
But
However high man may jump
Heaven is still out of his reach
His image can't be recreated
And all tools would come to nothing.
Even if one forges all the delicacy of creation at one place
It would still fall short of... one Heart.
No matter how many roses and China Roses were crushed
Not a drop of blood would come to life.

Whatever you write about man... becomes poetry
And it is only poetry that can equal life.
It is why, lady!
I made you into a poem
Unable to bring you back to life!

K GEETA

Missed Letter

Hi, pal! Howdy?
It's ages since you penned your last letter!
Nay, eons!!!
Moments we caressed our wounds
And the pep talk transcending epochs
Still lay under the creased folds.
Letter is
An elixir that fills
Every time you breathe
With doubled-up enthusiasm
It's an amazing leaf that relieves
Your heart with letters.

Hi, pal! Howdy?
How's home, children, neighborhood,
Loans, allowances, office, other mundane concerns?
Why make a call for festivals?
Send a message. That will do!
I am talking from the land-line,
So bye for now, lest bill would soar!
Where is the room for romance of language?
Diction itself drizzles down like spores

Blossoming blue sky
Touch of verdure grace
The sudden appearance of rainbow
The elegant rain-embedded cloud...

Be that cell-to-cell is free
Or the 'space-compressor' cell is a boon
Can you hear the beat of the heart
Behind that pronounced word?
Can it transmit the real musical
Symphony of the words aligned?

A letter is an epic
How many times ever it was re-licked!
It's an inerasable imprint of the heart
How many times ever you read it!!
It's an immutable form of the volatile word
Soul of the suppressed dreams...
Where had they gone
Those assertions of mutual welfare?
Where were 'Yours friendly's and
'Yours lovingly' leave takings?
'Hello', 'Hi' 'Bye' or "CU"
A smattering of courtesy
A scattering of scissored words strewn
And an asphyxiation of roots of words!

Hi, pal! Howdy?
Whenever I saw a letter stuffed into the door handle
My heart used to leap up... fledged!
Flashing in my memory
It used to spring an inadvertent smile
Over and again, whatever I did!!
Gee God! What happened!!!
Dull... dry ...dreary conversations, and
Angst shadowing the heart
Are 'cut' behind the 'bills'.
Many calls you can't afford to miss
Are anguishing as 'missed calls'

Pal! Dear pal!!
Letter is the only memento for life!!!
An oasis that quenches your thirst by degrees.
Life is immortal in a lively letter
That exhorts from past... when present frightens!

In the postman's bag, at best,
There are few LICs, 'On IGS's now,
And occasionally... few land-line bills.
Post card has become a relic of the past.
Not to speak of the Inland Letter
And the gloom-enveloped Envelopes.
No use ruing, it's our own undoing.

Alarms... clocks... letters...
Cell is now all-in-one!
Radios and cameras
Are on her morrow's menu!!
Pal!
There's no time to speak
Nor time to spare for the pen.
Hello! Hello!!
Pl mail this msg to all!!!
Land to land
Or cell to cell... no matter.
Pl. send this msg urgently.
See it's prominently displayed on cell screen
And the phone could hear:
"Here letter is on her deathbed."

Wakes on The Horizon ● A selection of poems

VIMALA

Beauteous Torture

When we reduce to
Measuring 34-24-35...
Growing pimples, losing hair,
And a size zero waistline
Become our perpetual worries...
When our life's sole aim becomes
Yearning for a beauteous body...
What a torture we suffer from!
Boring our ears and nose
We hang rings and nose-beads...
We daub and dab colors to our
Lips, fingers, eyes, and eye-brows...
We chain our neck, waist and feet
With varieties of shackles...
Pricking our body every minute
With tools of beauty
We mob the marts and malls to buy beauty...
Suspending varieties of clothing
To the body-hangers...
Applying oils
Curing it with pastes and turmeric packs,
We knead and knead our figures
Until they get parenthesized between figures...
No matter whether we smile, stroll, speak or sit
We crave for a pretentious beauty...
Cuddling, and cuddling snugly into the molds.

Translated from Telugu ● *NS Murty*   **93**

We believe this self-imposed torture
Is connate with us...

Whenever we look about ourselves
I am reminded of scare-crows of the corn fields
Stuffed with reed and grass...
Hollowed out of all that we are from ourselves
We look hollow like 'Egyptian Mummies'...
Even if muscles were measures
For our intellect, for our love, for our responses, and
For our emotions,
And we were reduced to mere bodies...
Then,
Even our bodies are not ours in the end...
What a hideous beauty is this!

Where beauty is a competition
Where beauty is a commodity
Let's hate that trading of beauty!
If beauty were inevitable for our existence,
Let's hate that very existence!

Where we are white-washed,
Erected like walls to hang photos on,
Reduced to decorated 'bulls'
And wounded with this compulsive 'beauteous torture'
There
Pals!
Let us call for a life
Nude,
Yes, as nude as we came out of our mother's womb,
Sans decorations...sans any measures of beauty!
Let us love that lack of beauty
Of crores of women
Who can't buy beauty,

Can't dab colors,
Can't rivet themselves between figures,
But labor ceaselessly... with
Lips split, hands hardened, hair disheveled,
Eyes tired, and could only don rags!
Let us love the beauty of labor and the human values!
Let us create a wonderful beauty for one and all...
And a world,
Replete with unaffected, natural beauty!

❖

One Midnight in San Francisco

"I left my heart in San Francisco..."
Tony Bennett was walking away singing crazily...

Still...
This dead of night
Over the blue firmament of San Francisco
And over the whiff of hazy black mist of cold winds.

2
Forgive me, Tony!
Madly believing your song to be true
I 'flotsam'med into this bay.
I am not able to hide under my eyelids
The cable cars you tied to stars
And your blue seas
I know you suspect my vision if I say
Your home looks to me
A walking skeleton donning lights.

3
For that matter, can any city be a home to anyone?
Who knows! As I was walking
Down the heart of downtown
It looks the drizzle of cold and fog
Has enveloped both the skin and the soul.
Of what hue and savor is indigence, you can see
Come here once Tony!

And play your song in that hue and savor.
You said you floated lonely somewhere, but

4
Hiding the dark truth of homelessness
Your song glitters like a funereal wreath
In the hunger's forest-fire of mortal frames.
That amber-colored sun
Is an untouchable... even here. Forever!

❖

SOWBHAGYA

I am Just Your Shadow

Everything in Nature is just made for you.
The whole creation is your excursing ground.
Planets of the cosmos are your play dolls.
Flowers just bloom for you and
Shower over you as you pass by.
You pick one of them and bless it
By decking it in your plait.
That azure sky and moonlight
Take shelter in your eyes.
Seasons walk in your footsteps
Keeping pace with your emotions.
And on the rim... I lie.

I was witness to every occasion when
Nature reflected itself through you.
I keep watch over your foot prints.
Weaving a garland with your looks, I follow you...
And buoy in ecstasy that has neither epoch nor end.

If you are generous to touch me, that would be my salvation.
Commend me... I shall become a flower.
Pray! Be kind to lock me up in your tresses.
Commend me...
I shall be a dove and land gently on your shoulder;
You just think of it...

I shall become a ring hugging your finger;
Or the golden chain lacing your neck, or
The smile adorning your lips,
Or, even become a stream of consciousness
And stroll within your thoughts.

❖

Rainbow

He is a magician of smiles.
Smiles so intoxicatingly sweet
As if he were an essence of
Aurum and moonshine
Milk and China rose
Honey and grape juice.

He turns all people at home
Around him in merry-go-round.
Waving the magic-wand of childy jargon
He rains fragrances of pleasures in spells
Giving a touch of music to his words
Arrests our attention making us his audience.

He is another creator of many exotic things.
A Viswamitra born into our family.
Whenever he thinks it meet
He creates a ravishing heaven on a rainbow
And presents it to our hands,
Blossoms as joy himself.
He is a walking nursery now.
A chirping on the flight.
Around that two-year-old boy
All of us run around
Like a bevy of herds and milkmaids of *Repalle*.

◆

Bangles of My Mother

Whenever I look at the bangle-less hands of my mother,
They remind me of a blank starless sky,
Barren branches sans flowers
Play before my bleary eyes.

Those bangles...
Which jingled with such inexpressible sweetness
When she put the childy me to sleep
Or bathed me or gave me breast caressing my head...
Still reverberate their echoes within me

I still remember those hands hurt and wounded
When father struck her in anger.
They used to break like pods of cotton
When she pounded chilies,
Broke firewood to faggots, or
As she washed the dish.

It was such a merry pastime in my childhood
To passionately collect those fragments and
Make colorful chains welding over lamp flame

Whenever the bangles sahib came and opened his box,
We children used to collect around him no sooner
Like a bevy of bees
And flew about that colorful world
Like butterflies struck with wonder and awe

Translated from Telugu • *NS Murty*   **101**

When mother donned a new sari some festive day and
Wore parrot-green or light red or violet bangles,
It looked as if rainbows have alighted on her hands

Whenever she wore stone bangles,
It seemed as if stars were studded on her celestial hands

When I rapturously counted my mother's bangles,
I felt they were my kin
And whenever I touched her bangles-box,
They greeted me from inside in their voice

Now, mother's bangles have grown silent
For, the last time when I witnessed
Her bangles being dashed against father's grave,
I think I heard
The rending of the sky into two
And bursting to pieces

Mother's bangles
Might have splintered to smithereens
But the bangles of my memories hold intact.
Her glistening hands, full of bangles,
Just as they were in my childhood,
Spread across my eyes... still

◆

SIKHAMANI

The Swan

Calendars and watches measure time
Sun measures the day, and Moon... the night.
Trees measure forests, and
Tides... the seas.
Wings of birds measure the expanse of the sky
While pupil of the eye measures horizons.
The mercury coated glass of the thermos flask
Measures the heat within the coffee.
Sacrifices measure revolutions
Tyagaraja's...@ the depths of music
Breast-milk measures the sweetness of motherhood.
Tears measure both ecstasy and agony
Eyes measure the dreams, while
The laughing lips... the joy.
Sensibilities measure experiences,
Experiences... the life.
Breath can measure both life and death.

But, there lies a principle
Eddying through them all.
If that snaps,
Separating qua milk from aqua
The swan* flies off to frontiers unknown.

@ *Tyagaraja (1767-1847) was one of the greatest composers of Carnatic Music,
the classical music of South India.*

* *In the poetic parlance a Swan is supposed to have been endowed with the skill to
separate milk from water.*

KALEKURI PRASAD

For an Ounce of Self-Respect

I don't know when I was born
But I was annihilated on this very land
And since, passing through the cycle of birth and death.
I know nothing about the Theory of Karma
But I was rising over and over again
On the very soil I was ceasing.
Melded into this expanse,
My land has become the Ganga-Sind plateau
When tears overwhelmed in my eyes
The rivers of this land have become perennial.
When elements oozed from my veins
This country has become prosperous yielding plenty
Eons before, I was Sambooka
And twenty two years before
I was Kancikacharla Kotesu,
I was born at Kilvenmani
Karamcedu and Neerukonda.
But now, the name that the hardened feudal cruelty
Tattoos on my heart with its sharp ploughshare
Is Chunduru.
From hence, Chunduru is no longer a noun
But stands for a pronoun.
Every heart is a Chunduru now...
An open un-healing cancerous abscess.
I am a wound of the masses
And a mass of hurts.

For generations immemorial
I have been a slave in a free country
Subjected to insults and abuses
Rape and torture.
I raise my head to uphold my ounce of self-respect.
In a reign of hubristic, filthy rich, arrogant blood
I just live to assert my protest
And for the sake of existence, I die every moment.
Don't call me a sufferer
I am immortal!
I am immortal!! I am immortal!!!
To spare this world of its riches
I swallowed the venom of famine;
Standing the somersaulting dawn upright
I kicked the Sun on his face;
I voice the words of anger
Tempered in the furnace of my heart.
Stop! Spare your words of compassion
Shed no tears for me.
I am not a sufferer
But a fluttering flag of contempt and disdain.
Pray! Shed no tears for me.
If it is possible for you
Bury me at the centre of the city.
I grow into a great grove of bamboo
To play the tunes of life perpetually.
Put my dead body
On the cover page of this country.
Into the pages of history
I penetrate like a promising future.
Quelled in the battle of torches
I will be born again on this land.

VINNAKOTA RAVI SANKAR

The Ultimate Survivor

Gradually
Life becomes
A reconciliation to death.
Instead of pigeons, now
Lapwings carry messages.
The smiling faces
Of the childhood group-photo
Leave one by one
Searching for their own.
Not only the actors,
Even the audience recede
One after another.
There will be nobody left
On either side,
To share tears
For the tragedy on the stage.
Besides shedding its leaves,
The deciduous Family Tree
Sheds its roots as well
Intermittently.
After all tangles are disentangled
And all strings are snapped,
A wizened spiritless frame remains
Like the sole thread
Connecting it to the Nature.

◆

BVV PRASAD

Homesickness

When there was no ruffle
All ripples hid under the lake
And water nestled in water rather nicely.
When there was no streak of light
All shadows ducked behind night
And darkness reposed in downy darkness
When everything was calm
All sounds dissolved in silence,
And serenity had spread out stately.

Then,
Where did we all hide
When there was no being?
And what had happened to the whole creation?
Just as concentric ripples emanate
From a placid pond once a stone is thrown into it
Some inexplicable ripples of anguish
Have surfaced after raising these questions.
Along with this wintry fog rises
An anxiety to reach the place of origin
To fill the air and the surrounding firmament.

Translated from Telugu ● NS Murty   **107**

AFSAR

On the Banks of River Kaveri

1

A pining...

For not having drowned like a paper boat
When you were impregnably brimming over the banks;
For having failed
To play like a pearl of water
On the sickle of your waist
When the first signs of youth blossomed over there;
For not sharing a piece of firmament
Standing at the threshold of your teary look

2

Kaveri!
You are now an abridged version of your own epic;
And I...
A worn out boat on your attenuating banks...
A childhood running into the crimps
Of those aureate saris drying up over there on your sands

3

As for the contentment, well, there is.
There is that satisfaction that you lie here
On the hem of my cilia.

4

But,
What I came here for
Is to anchor oceans in my eyes;
What I came here for
Is to stream around your wizened ribs in ripples.

5

Isn't it Kaveri?

Living With a Computer

My dad has ten heads, and has ten brains for each head
So he bought me a husband lavishing the money.
His brains have earned committing every conceivable irregularity.
We bought a computer spending lakhs, in turn.
My mother has thousand tongues
Only that she did not have time to get literate.
Yet, there is not a word in the language she did not know
That is why she tom-toms that all the software in America
Is at the mercy of my husband.

"You are my second wife," he said on the first-night itself
Of course, before I could recover from my start,
He reassured me saying "computer" was his first wife.
"Let him be whatever machine he wants,"
Was my blissful ignorance.
Going to America first was my primary concern.

After everything was packed including the pickle bottles
He came home like a trimmed lotus from a pond
Hanging his head holding a pink slip.

Ultimately we reconciled to leading our hi-tech life in Hyderabad.
The car presented by my dad lies always at his office parking lot
I have to attend any function all alone
Hey, what is your hubby's address? I give his mail id.
Come on! How can I talk to him? I give his chat site.
It was I who remained ultimately sans any identity.

I have to rejoice on my own if I buy jasmine.
If he had married computer, I am living with it.

How long shall this lust for money last?
Half the earnings go towards buying
Insurance for tax saving, and for bribing.
Perhaps, the word "husband" means one
Who visits in sleep and hies before wife wakes up!
My man, who never turns up till date changes;
Whenever he explores me... at last... not now... tomorrow.

❖

KAVI YAKOOB

Only One Life

You have but only one life.
Whether you are glad or gloomy;
Win or vanquished;
Rejoice or repent;
There is but just one life!

Within its scope,
Desires pile up like tamarind sprigs
Words course through the pathways to reach papers;
The slumbering letters
Lie drowsing on the finger tips dreaming of wakening
And the enduring yearning of bodies
Swims across the night with aching feet.

There is some consolation and some consternation;

Some instances and some intentions
Beam and blow out like the hands of a clock

Would anybody ask about your wellbeing?
Would they bless you with something?

What more anyone would?
What else can anybody ask beyond this
Than asking, and cleansing themselves?
For that matter, what can anybody give?

There is but one life that won't re-start,
And for sure, there is never a second stint.

❖

ADURI SATYAVATHI DEVI

Oh This, After All!

I fancy I know you
But before I could confirm it
The context you created changes.
While I would be debating myself
The way to comprehend you
You recede into oblivion in ringlets.
Just watching you and bewildering
I liken your receding to the flow of a river
But, it is a world hemmed between two banks.
I rejoice comparing you to the sky
Yet, it occasionally pales out
Seeming helplessly leaning over cosmic horizons.
Trying to find the shades of sea in you
I want to rest content reconciling.
Isn't it another ferocious beauty within bounds?
You immeasurable, incomparable Time!
Magic on the move!
Momentum unconquerable by any force!
You are restless and not for a second take rest.
In that marathon run
You don't even throw a sly look.
Time! When I come in your speeding way
How many thousands of hands
You stretched to hug me dearly!
Drowned in how many symphonies!
We run after one another endlessly
In our play of hide-and-seek.

❖

Translated from Telugu ❧ *NS Murty*

BVV PRASAD

When Heart Takes Over

Why do we witness those rare drops of tear
In a mother's eyes when her son,
Who constantly chafes at her for nothing,
Touches her feet for a blessing?

Why do tears stream out from her pale eyes
When you sincerely apologize your wife
Pleading guilty for the hurt?

Why do the eyes of a father get bleared
When he recalls the love-filled talk of his young kids
Who display rare concern for money saying:
"Not now, daddy, they might cost more"?

Why a wet film of love flutters
Like moist wind, between them,
When a taciturn father keeps awake for his son
Who travels distances to reach home past midnight?

Why do our eyes get wet,
And we feel a lump in our throat
When we notice those rare acts of humanity?
Or, when someone acknowledges
That vanishing creed of good deeds?
Or, when we win over,
And help others triumph over
Hearts with graceful gestures?

Why life becomes so serene
And an alluvial silence embraces two people
Every time the heart prevails over
Their intellectual aberrations, and,
Apparent physical strengths
Melding them into a trail of tears?

May be... then, we are
Catching up with ourselves delving deep;
Or, looking at our revealing spiritual selves
Rinsing off all temporal sullies;
Or, awakening into our godly path
Which we have long deserted and digressed from.

VIMALA

Butterflies

Whenever I forget dreaming about,
A Butterfly comes and rests on my eyelids with compassion,
And gifts me
With a dream and a smidgen of poetry.

Losing the Sarangi of Faith and the flutter of moonbeams
On the banks of Vaitarani*, and renouncing everything,
When I walk away like Sufi mendicant
A butterfly landing on my forearm flapping its rainbow-wings
Initiates conversation with me like a good old friend

When I watch idly the coquettish waves on the blue seashore
Or, the voluptuous clouds wafting aloft on the azure sky,
A butterfly courses from nowhere
To spray honey over my lips.

When life loses its fragrance,
A band of butterflies
Dwelling on the arbor of Goldflowers,
Descend on my book-of-life
Like multi-hued letters.

Whenever the darkness of
Tenuous humanity frightens me,
A 'tiara'ed butterfly settles slowly
And prognoses like a priestess of the Oracle
Floodlighting my way all through.

When I pen a poem on the cheeks of Time,
A butterfly flies down ever so delicately
To settle on my peacock-plume pen

I go in search of an island of butterflies.
I was, perhaps, a butterfly myself in my last life.
There's a chest of butterfly-tattoos on my chest.
Today, I started off searching for those butterflies
Which bestowed wings to my thoughts
And dabbed them with every hue.

* *The infernal river that souls are supposed to cross after death.*

❖

She Repeats Herself

She met me
When she was nineteen

From then on
She was completely known

Know not how she guessed
That I wanted to see her life
Before I met her

She blessed me with a girl child

She said
She would keep the child till she is eighteen
And send her

She met me
When she was nineteen

◆

SIVA REDDY

It's Difficult to Stand-Up

It's difficult to stand up.

You don't realize...
When you live giving a damn.

You don't realize...
But it's hard to stand up...
'Enduring everything
Yet, remaining unshattered' is exacting.
It's easy to crack and
Collapse shattered
And easier to scatter like scared looks.

What it takes, after all, to blow out?
But, it's hard to inflame like a faggot.
But then, how difficult it is to burn!
Donning flame like attire and
Walking swinging hands like branches
Upon hills, across oceans,
Among valleys, along meadows
Above abysses, over summit tops...
How arduous it is to walk with ease
Wearing a peacock's plume in the crown
Floating above the ground.

It would be pleasing to the onlookers
Even amusing and entertaining.
But, only the walker can feel

Translated from Telugu ▪ NS Murty   **119**

The scorching under the feet
The boils rending within
The vortices and volcanoes
Moistening eyes and melting colors.
He would hole them out between folds of the pages

We can't get a clue.
We will be looking at his eyes and his feet.
Standing upright with grit and gumption
He would walk away,
Looking conquered or about to conquer the world.

And in his wakes follow
A few cyclones and a few rainbows.

◆

HRK

God

When the child had drawn a picture
The Sky was floored,
The Stars blushed, and as
Some mottled polka dots patterned,
The Moon let out a hearty laugh.

Mazarine-hue water, yellow-scaled fish, butterflies,
Unknown and unimaginable worlds... and what not
They embodied whatever she desired...

Why do stars and moon love whatever a child does?
Why should the sky stand in awe? Or,
Why do the worlds follow like cows charmed by flute?

Treading over damp papers wetted with teary colours,
I went out holding the child's finger and asked the sky...
Clouds that morphed to varied shapes
When somebody tossed them up effortlessly
Grinned and admitted to the Air:
We are not sure if there is god or not;
But, if He were to be there, He would be there as a child.

From then on,
I never had any issue with anybody... even with god.
If ever there was any issue,
It was only with the un-child-like official...
With the etymology of good and evil, and
With the absurd stories in the name of religion.

❖

SKYBAABA

A Pall of Soil

Informed about my death, people flocked around
I was listening to the truths about me in their conversations...

Friends and relatives are hurrying paying their last visit.
How unbearable the last looks are!

They washed me carefully limb by limb
It was only my mother who did it so when I was a child.

They rested me on my back...
If somebody could tell I like sleeping on my sides.

They were applying attar to my body...
How could I tell them I liked my body odor more?

They were wailing their hearts out...
Everybody forgot that I could not stand somebody weeping.

They covered me with a white *Kaphan*
How many colours I ran after while alive!

They were competing to give shoulder to the *Janaajaa*
I could not distinguish between the known and unknown

I always used a fresh and clean bed sheet...
Now there was this soily pall.

How awfully I exploited this soil
Yet it blessed me with a place in its lap.

A heap of flowers was razed over me...
I was not sure... if this were heaven or earth

◆

AFSAR

My Heart Coos

1

Yours is
A rattling voice that flows with a tremble...
An agitated river...
Collecting itself ...much like a feverish child under a blanket.
Lowering a pregnant hovering cloudlet to earth,
You flash like lightning bowing on its splitting vein.
Shrinking into silence like her ... a disquiet Godavari.
For the last time before snapping,
In the wellspring of your voice,
There's a feverish yearning, stumbling for life
In the grating of your words.

2

There's a song storming within,
Consummating a rumbling cloud and a parched heart
Raining on the bouldered city,
Befriending light in the night,
And in the day, concealing darkness within.

3

There's nothing to write, till the humming of the heart ceases
Not sure if it were fear,
Like when an uncharted train passes through a tunnel.

4

O, My Deliverer!

Don't I hold my breath and grip my body in my fist?

Don't stop, don't stop your song,

Till my blind run comes to an end.

K GODAVARI SARMA

Rilke

You like questions.

The more,
The more it's hard
To find answers
To those questions.

And like them the most
If there are no answers to them at all!

Like rooms locked up
And languages you can't make out
They attract you to the extreme.
And you sing in those tongues
Incarcerated in those rooms.

Rilke!
You are an answerless question.
Is it why I like you more?

❖

ADURI SATYAVATHI DEVI

Care of

When the letters are at heart
And heart itself becomes a poem,
Poesy founts streams of elixir.
When poetry is the altaltissimo
Of all life's yearnings
Mind turns halo
Swaying a cascade of tunes.
While rowing across life's seaways
In the boat of poetry
The cottage of universe,
Without walls or veils becomes visible.
Vision elevates to the skies
Enveloping the earth as the invisible ether.
This effulgent canopy
Moves in the direction of splendour
That all mankind hails.
Sinking in the sea of humanity
As epochs and events
The names with glittering wings
Open-up exquisite sensuous dawns
On the curtain of time.
Then, and only then
Poem stands-out
As tall as life itself.

◆

SOWBHAGYA

Mirror Image

In a still-water-like mirror
Rolling its eyes once,
Rollicking with laughter next,
Motionless now
And effervescing with activity in no time
Dithers your image.

In the full-length mirror up there,
Lies your reflection.
Hiding from its view
And stealing glances with it... secretly stand I.
Oooooh! That gleaming rosy countenance
Is so inviting to kiss.
Sweet melodies from
That graceful helical body flow unto me.

How fortunate is the mirror!
You enter into its lifeless heart like a dove.
And there, in freedom, fly with abandon.
I will be glued to you.
You will be so unmindful of your treasures.
Perhaps, when you are cynosure of all eyes,
You need pay no attention to your self.

I enter the mirror... invisible
And watch your aural beauty from close.
I take it into my hands...

Translated from Telugu ● NS Murty

That dream? No, not.
Chrysanthemum? No, not.
That beauteous and blissful face? Yes,
And passionately plant kisses
On the bewildered lips and those lovely eyes.

Unable to stand the brunt of my emotion,
The mirror breaks... and you disappear.
I start... in search of you.

◆

SIKHAMANI

The Tree

If you have any sense of the word,
Tree is an open book.

If you dare to look at your own reflection
Tree is a full-length dressing mirror.

If you have sensibilities within
Tree is a sea on high tide.

If you observe mere trunk, boughs and twigs
Inflorescence and frondescence
You are just a Duryodhana.
But if you can mark the eye of the little bird hiding
Amidst the valley of verdant foliage
You become an indomitable Arjuna.

Never look down upon fallen leaves.
They are passionate martyrs
Who sacrificed their lives
For the sake of coming generations.
They are the unforgettable yesterdays
Which bequeath a legacy to the todays.

Did you ever watch an old leaf floating down?
Listened to the clack of a dry twig?
The quotidian visiting bird never finds
The flowers of yesterday
Or the fruits of the day before.

The light in the day
And moonshine at night
Acquaint themselves anew with the tree every day.

The Tree you see is not "The" Tree, for truth.
It is the occult code of life that enlivens you and me.
Like a miner in a gloomy pit,
Exploring us unawares from depths within.
The verdure to the leaf
And ruddiness to the blood
Have come only from there!

◆

K GEETA

His Hug

There are downs in his hug
That can fan out all temporal afflictions.
While the six passions steadily subside, only
Reassurance rules the roost.

Many a time
My heartbreaks
Flowed down his falcate neck,
And on his prickly little bony chest
My cheeks washed their wounds.
Like a woe-less plain
Presenting itself in a vacuous world,
All of a sudden
There treasures in his little hands
A fearless plain one stumbles upon from nowhere.

Can any heart love me as hearty and pure?
Or, being born my babe,
Can make me a babe, in turn, other than him?
Assuaging my life's angst,
Dressing my dreamy hours
And sweeping aside with the dexterity of his hand
My shattered moments of grief,
Can anybody other than him
Bring the light of happiness to my eyes?

In his embrace lies
An unending expanse of enduring maternity.
Did anybody hug me like that ever before?
Did anybody run his hand over my head
Draining all my pangs and pains off?
Did anybody dry my eyes
Becoming a father and mother same time?

Assigning his five years to his mom
And growing to a love-incarnate
From his broke-mother's agonies,
He dressed her wounds
With his caressing kisses.
As if he were garlanding me with his heart
He ran into my hands, hugged me,
Drew my head unto him,
And resurrected me
From agonies time and again.

Why not?
There are stately steps
Of assured peace in his hug
Enough to crown me
For thousand lives.

◆

VINNAKOTA RAVISANKAR

Principle of Life

It matters little even if you have no friends
But, you can't make life without an enemy.
A man without a rival born
Is as vegetable as a brain-dead.

With all that, it's just a game.
And like in every game,
More than that of your team
The role of your rival counts most.

Man might wriggle out of umpteen bonds
But never the snares of success and reverses.
Man is yet to invent an intoxicant
More headier than success.

Man is a strange wild beast:
It vanquished the forest
But, surrendered to its heart.

Whatever the new equations be
Rivalry is a constant factor,
The only variable is... the rival.

Translated from Telugu ● *NS Murty*

AFSAR

I Have No Nat

I am some limb
Lingering under a hollow head
You never told me
Where I originated from
Who brought me up or
Why I was partitioned exactly in '47
Cutting off, or appropriating each limb of God
Else, looting them for yourself,
You did not leave anything for me.

I am an ethereal shadow,
A soul disposed of secretly over the wall,
I am wandering about countries.
Thought each one of them my own and
Each station and every door mine
But, no bumblebee gives out my address.
Some vermilion hands
Ploughed away the land under my feet
The dust from those temple towers knocked down
Piles up on my fluttering body entombing it.
Palling my eyes with eyelids

Everybody rends my cool body
Snatching his pound of flesh.
My body is now an Al Kabir!
I am dropping down dead on the gory Bombay streets
Unable to identify my own cadaver.

I am an enigmatic junction, where
Nobody knows what he is heading up to.
I am an inhabitant of this vacuous world, for truth
But, always an exile wherever I might live.
Sinking one half of me in darkness,
I illusion the other half is all bright
Diving into my inner vortices
I kill the soul of Time each second
I ask for no kingships and no kin-shares
I have no language
To ask for my veins to deracinate.
I am satisfied with some semblance of shelter on earth
No matter there's no room to bury me beneath.
The land I live is sanctimonious to me,
Pray! Don't cast me off somewhere, like a desecrated cloth.
Not with forty-seven
I ask you to divide me by myself
My rejoices, my wails, my insults and my suspicions
These molestations and murdering of me
Are not mine, and mine alone... but yours too.
Please don't abominate the amniotic fluid of my mother.
You foes who divide and rule!
You can't sever me into two.
Nor, can you blow my pupils off.

❖

When it's Time to Leave

Neither you want to leave
Nor do I want to send you off.
Not that we are aware
That it is an ineluctable choice
Helplessly stand
You
And I.
Yet, with a hope
Like the dawns…
And the endless tomorrows...
Eagerly awaiting
That miracle
Which stops you from leaving.

We Don't Want This Tradition

Tradition is not a thunderbolt.
Yet it has incinerated thousands of lives.

Tradition is not darkness.
Yet, it has thrown into immeasurable precipices

Tradition is not a despot
Yet, it has reduced history to armchair fiction

Tradition is not a prison.
Yet, it has confined expanses of unsullied waters
Into the weir of threaded ewer.

The exhausted palanquin-bearers of tradition
Who confuse their deep sighs for cooing, are inured
To donning their conscience, and doffing their clothes.

❖

The Delimiting Line

Even living together is a crime.

Besides, there are unknown dividers
Between every exercise and activity.
And amidst those unerasable lines
A newborn's life starts,
Without its knowledge,
With a question mark.

And the five-year old Sahir
When he delineates
Father's side with Allah, and
Mother's side with a different god
He embarks upon his life
With the same question once more.

Pity!
This child's life finds it hard
To break through the rusted framework of religions.
In his playful times and tunes, conduct, reflexes and reactions
These two houses are two inalienable boundaries.
It's not a crime to love to wear a vermillion on the forehead,
Or to efface it on either side of the boundary.

But settled habits and practices
Like benchmarks of life...
"Sarasvati! I bow before you..."
"Allah Hu Akbar!"

Fissure conjugal obligations of life.
From the teasing names of religions
To the pervading roots of prohibitions
I remain a masjid, and she remains a temple.
And I wonder what tabernacle I should erect
For this poor child as a mark of our marriage?

No philosopher shall assure
Whether or not we can reach a religionless state.
Neither atheists dispense with vermillion, bangles and turmeric
Nor rationalists and pagans, religious symbols.
Perhaps, like blood,
Religion has also established its right over this body.
Lines are drawn between two states
Between body and religion
Between body and its affinities
Between body and its emotions...
It's an endless... warp... of... delimiting lines!

Spectral-hued Hope

Hope
Which from that endless abysmal strains of grief,
Blossoms as clear chrysanthemum of smiles
On the lips of a babe

Hope
That eons-familiar mystic astral-drizzle
That rains unseen at night
On the expansive silent seas of darkness

Hope
Which walks with green grassy step(pie)s
Through the sand storms of Saharan Desert

Hope
That lukewarm bonfire warmth of faggots
Kindled on the solidified icy Arctic seas

Hope
That streak of lightning
Like the glittering cardinal rays of rising sun
That kiss the earth on its head

Hope
That comes floating on the chariot
Of wafting cloud currents

Hope
That lilting little cool moonbeam
Advancing on the swing of crescent moon

Hope
That animate primitive dormant dreams in me
Touching my dreamy eyes ethereally like peacock plumes,

Hope
That enduring water-spring amidst the heaps of sandy debris
Annals of destructive degenerate human civilizations

Hope
That pleasant seizure of desire
That showers fragrances of green champak
On the lacerated life

Hope
That warm soothing embrace of a mother
To a wailing kid vanquished in his play

Hope
That inviting tintinnabulation of anklet bells
In the profound silence of
Encircling aimless cul-de-sac,

Hope
That spec of spark that lights life eternally

Hope
That pulsating life of man who unveiled a supreme wonder

Hope
That din of gallant resistances by the common men

Hope
That Morning Star which kindly leads the way
When the earth under the feet suddenly gives in

Hope!
Come! Settle on my sails of dreams
Becoming a spectral hued butterfly!

Translated from Telugu ● NS Murty

SILALOLITA

The Tiger

All the blessings for longevity, and happiness
Shall be confined to age four or five.
They may blossom to the same twig of a plant
But each of the flowers meets a different fate:
Clear barriers, destinies, veils of fidelity,
Adorning the bode and putting on lingering shades of blushing
Are inseverable fetters to womanhood

That follow up to the grave.
Wanting recognition
And even a smack of compassion
Femininity fatigues in the identity crises.

Amidst shades of swelling tears
I must touch up the cheeks with powdery smiles
And act what behooves of me with alertness before all.
The moment I open the book, like any other sibling,
The younger brother starts crying,
The elder fellow roars at me,
Father knits his brows
And there would be no end to mother's errands;
The household chores grip me like a python.
Only the sleep that makes no discrimination of sex
Mercifully visits the work-weary eyes.
Yet, I can't appropriate sleep like others
As days reduce to encumbrances
Under several masters.

I would be tethered to a post for display.
Men shall come and go endlessly
Inspecting and testing me, my body and my skills.

Nobody gets satisfied with this body and its worth
I will be yearning for a change of place;
Father who fails to balance me with money-weights
Starts reviling me with synonyms for daughter;
Mother corks up all teary-springs at kitchen's threshold;
And brothers look at me... as an impending calamity.

How long can I stand donning the veil of smiles?
I love the times I can stand on my feet.
My battle is ahead
With the tiger that ensnares me.

Translated from Telugu ● NS Murty   **143**

ANISETTI RAJITA

Food-pot

A mother rests reassured
When there is a food-pot in her home.
If there is mother moving around in the house
It amounts to having a food-pot at home.

That mother may have farm and fields;
May even have a government job;
But she shall not have a husband
That would toil and feed her...
Only one that would eat, beat and swear at her.
Yet, when her children are at home,
She feels so contented.

That mother may not be a literate
Or may not be in the know of current fashions.
All that she knows is the hard labour
She got accustomed to
Since she was young and fledgling.
Even while she was a lamb,
They thrust adulthood on her
And crowned her with life's imperatives.

No matter whether it's her fathers' home
Or her father-in-law's
That poor woman has to labour for a morsel
Exerting like the tethered ox of an oil-ghanni;
Ignoring her own hunger

She earns bread for the family
And grinds herself all through years.

She is a downy wing
That warmly embraces the family abode;
A motherly hen to her chicks
Always on the alert and protecting;
She becomes a small kerosene lamp
Driving darkness away from the gloomy home
And glitters like a warm sunshine at dawn.

She reduces to a food-pot
That was rolled out of earth
And burns on fire;
Becomes a cornucopia to the hungry family
Satiating their hunger
Cooking pot after pot on the stove!
She thus drags her life...
Burning like an incense stick.

NIRMALA GHANTASALA

The Accident

Whenever I lift a morsel to my mouth...
A bleeding brawn appears 'fore my eyes,
Whenever I hear the sound of a horn...
I hear
A silent wail of a mother with a lump in her throat.
'Accident is a mishap'
Defines the 'Learn English in 30 days' book
'A sudden unexpected occurrence' says the world at large...
But, accident means...
The rattling of the mind witnessing in front,
A life struggling to cease or no...
Burden of a freaky sin that follows us to our last breath...
An egregious guilt we can't shed to the end of our lives.

We never know until that moment
That we love so much... the innocent... the hapless...
And the boys that run across the road!
And lesser still
That the innocent, the hapless, at the threshold of death
Love us as dearly!
That with no trace of vengeance they admit their trespass, and
Stretch their hands to the cool hug of death in despair!

It's an insufferable embarrassment
When people enquire about you unmindful of the felled nearby,
More than the grief that simmers for them,
The compassion of the victim's parents touches deep within,
If you forget for a moment...

The Supreme Being... act of Sin...
Ephemeral life... a moment's lapse
FIR... additional judge... and the rest...

The boy felled running for a stalk of sugarcane...
Is a spear dug deep in my spine for life...
The one who attained divinity
Bathing in blood without batting an eyelid...
Battling to bid his last adieu by hand to this metallic world
That wrote his childy-impishness off at eight...
Is
The truth... shadow... charge...
Crime and punishment and everything for me!!!

Do you have licence?
Yes! (Thank god, I have!)
Did you renew it?
Yes, I did. I did. (Thank God! I am saved!)
Wrong route?
Root is wrong! (Power and pelf play Ping-Pong with life)
That's not what I say, is the route wrong?
Everything is wrong with our roots
Where things bend for the tinkle of a coin!

Suffering hell for four days
He spilt over the lifeless eyes of his father
And was lost cuddled up in his unkempt beard!
It was he, who capsized in the dried up tears of his mother!
He was the mash in the potholes of the road!!!
Darting truth into my heart, and
Appropriating to himself the blame...
That he ran across the road... and,
Reassuring that I need not have to
Run around to beat the rap,
Ginning himself of the body
He bravely walked away in search of other worlds!

Translated from Telugu ● *NS Murty*

What is it we are left with for the rest of our lives
When he takes all our courage away?
Unable to wail hollow
Over the sentence for an uncommitted crime,
Unable to milk loans to the dear ward, unrelated
Towards his ward charges at hospital;
What else could I do... than to freeze in my heart's mortuary
The 'kin'ly soul that bade me last good bye?
Putting to sleep at midnight those pairs of searching eyes
That dared not ask if he was dead, with food-packets
I warmed my cooled night-out tea-cup with hiccups...
Balancing in dark, innocent life against a long inventory of loans!

Oh, Boy!
We...
Who poked our eyes with the finger that steers the power-wheel
Who choked you to death with your own statement
Whom sleep eschews to draw near today, and
Whose hearts were poke-marked with your death...
Cry hoarse that we aren't at fault,
Ready ourselves to light candles at your funeral!

O, you boy!
Who ran across our path all of a sudden!
Oarsman of your family boat of sustenance unto the last!
The dismal shadow of sin that trails me to my eternal rest!
A life-size blood stain on my plate!
These hands are so helpless trudging the cross across
That they can't even pay their last homage to you!!!

AFSAR

Death Indeed

Death is not
Starvation
Neither Tsunami
Nor cessation of heart beat...

When a promise made hides behind equivocation
When a profile coldly vanishes into the back, or
When a man is banished into eternal silence...
That is... a veritable death.

Murders
Suicides
Abortions
Are not death.

When the cherished faith you so covetously held
Mercilessly bites and hurts you deep

When an unfamiliar hand
Turns into a murderous knife
By pinning a wound to the heart like a rose
That... that is death indeed.

❖

Translated from Telugu ❖ *NS Murty*   **149**

KONDEPUDI NIRMALA

Quick Mail Service

The letter you posted six months back
Was delivered to me yesterday.
Never mind the delay.

Compared to the prisoner-like Independence
Freed some thirty-nine years ago,
Which did not reach home as yet,
It has reached far sooner.

Enough if you own
A voice to applaud
And the courage to denounce.

Even a faint moonlight
That liberally casts on our face is much better
Than the bright electric light
That works under controls.

◆

Knowing About Knowing

My father used to say those days:
It's not enough if you write poetry,
You must have some wisdom.

I still feel
Wisdom might be useful for everything else
But what you need to write poetry
Is some innocence of the mind
And a compassion towards fellow beings.

Very recently
A post-modernist commented:
OK, you write well,
But you are not an intellectual poet.
"So what?" I looked up, my mannerism
Somewhat suggestive of
Challenging him rounding up my moustache.

Yesterday my wife had also said:
Of what use are these scribblings?
You don't know anything. Better keep quiet.
But how to convince her
That even I know that I know nothing?
May be she would come to know
After noticing my happiness within.

And ultimately, today
Even my children have commented:

Translated from Telugu ● *NS Murty*

Daddy! You know nothing.
The only difference being,
They said so in English...

I yearn to know what this 'thing' is
When so many people say I know it not.

In a way, perhaps,
It is an endeavor to know the know not
Be it Life!
Or Poetry!!

ADURI SATYAVATHI DEVI

A Foundling

A screaming unwanted child when he was born
An offshoot of municipal rag-ring
A penalty paid by some innocence
For a trespass or somebody's necessity...
The stains of blood over him
Won't betray any addresses.
When delicate etiquettes had turned their backs
Throwing blankets of silence on his first cries,
Like 'compassion' had walked down...
That motherhood was still alive...
A pair of old hands from a street-end hut
Cuddled that dirty baby
Resurrecting humanness
And fostered him with love.

When on one stormy day
The curtain was downed
On an already tattered old life
The lone destitute, to the entire street,
Had become a sweetmeat
That we smacked our lips at.
Giving him the leftovers of our food,
Worn-out clothing gratis
His childhood
We have been seasoning our lives with.
Without him, our days won't take-off
Be it for marketing or

For leaving children at school.
Our polished shoes and creased clothing
Shine under the charity of his labour.
Whenever he meets me square in the eyes... smiling...
With a sense of guilt
I shrink to a mustard seed.

Are Sons an Investment?

"Do you suppose sons are an investment?"
Asked a son of his father.
Nonplussed at the sudden question,
Unable to find an answer, the father
Murmured within "What are parents then?"

Why do you expect
Everything to happen the way you want
And everybody to grow the way you desire?

When everything is social, and
Is defined by context
Answers won't be as easy as the questions.
It's very difficult to separate a strand unsnapped
From a tangled spool of thread.

True
I admit economic root of every relation-
But then, can we define them all
In economic jargon?

No.
Human relations are not so simple
As to be amenable to economic lingo.

Trying to define recondite responses and reactions
Would be like pulling out a tree from earth
And trying to 'bonsai' it in a glass of water.

As you said,
If one were to use the economic argot
Parents ARE Capital
And children grow on it like interest.

Children won't remain children
They too become parents.

◆

KOPPARTHY

Hieroglyphics

Ruins of Harappa speak inaudibly...
In the revelry of Aryan assemblies
The Ganges plateau trills with great cities...
The imprints of three hard feet
That walked over the Aborigine
Slipped from "Purusha Sookta" are marked ..
A severed thumb would be found in Dandakaranya.
Only the middle path in philosophy
Bears the foot prints of Tathagata...
Asoka stands like a stone inscription in Dhammapadam...
In the backdrop of Mahayana degenerating to Hinayana
'Advaita' stands peerless...
A pariah with a bell hanging to his neck
Desecrates the golden era of Gupta's...
The Emperor who gifts everything away is left
With just his clothes on, at the confluence of two rivers...
The mysticism of Sufi tradition
Binds a Muslim Emperor like a sacred thread...
The glorious facet of Prabandhas' excellence
Shall not betray the other facet of farmers
Crossing the borders of the Land of Jewels
Unable to cough up rents
And put up with the atrocities of feudal Poligars...
Everything will be in disarray...
Only one man

Questions, angers, grieves, and chastises
And walks away unclad spinning out his poems.

When the doors to land-ways are shut
Ships make high water-ways over the seas...
A drizzle develops into a storm
Farmers become partners in agriculture,
And the partners, in turn, to farm-workers,
Carts become ships
But never shall ships reduce to carts.

A Saint walks a marathon on foot to hold
A handful of sea salt in his fist...
Properties get divided
Distinction between white and black would be erased
'Old City' suffers the consequences of Chunduru.

The dialogue between the past and the present continues
No traces of the mud-houses shall remain
However,
The shadow under the lamp
Continues drawing hieroglyphics.

Habit

Sometimes, we should get out of our daily rut
And declare independence from the rote routine.

For a change, we should leave the vehicle and go on foot;
Greet for the first time the unknown person
We regularly meet on the road
Forget all the cares and sleep by day and wake through the night.

We should scan the skies from end to end
And see if god had made any changes to its measure of late
By re-counting the stars to tally with our childhood numbers.

Sitting alone and laughing
We should check if our laughter needs any repair; and
To ensure that we can still shed tears, we should wail for a while.

But above all, we should think why we should do anything at all,
And coolly observe what happens if all imagination ceases.

I am not sure if the world is a great myth or not, but habit is;
If it seizes us like numbness
We will be oblivious to the pleasures and pains of life.
When we can wriggle out of its grasp, it feels like... rebirth.

To perceive the delight of existence, we should live habit-free
And stand on our own, without relying on any routine
The only permissible habit, if at all, is... accustoming to life.

Like the flood sweeping with it everything that loses its ground,
It's enough we can inhibit habit, life carries us afloat with it.

❖

K GEETA

His 20th Birthday

Are these the same kid-like hands
That entwined my neck till the other day?!
It seems some alien bony youth
Has entered into my cherub.

Are they the same balloony cheeks
Protesting against taking food in anger?
Somebody has meticulously carved that tender moustache
Over the enduring smiley face of the new youth.

Is he the same little boy who pleaded:
"Mommy, I won't go to school today!"
Poor me! He doesn't look aside from his table
Preparing for entrance examinations into the wee hours.

Is he really the same endlessly talkative child?!
The youth has grown reticent
And for hours on his looks are glued silently to his laptop.

Are they the same listlessly wailing eyes
Craving for mother within the four walls of his hostel room?
Somebody has cast a charm petrifying him
Bestowing looks of apathy

Is he the same capering hart that
Never stood still at a place for even one minute?!
Without informing where he is dashing off
He zooms past on his bike, this leading stag of wild deers.

On his birthday, every time,
I relive the fleeting agony of my first labour
And recall the tiny batting eyelids
Of a marvellous creature that has just opened its eyes.

A confident smile that smacks of conquering the world
And an elderly mien exhibiting civility and etiquette.
In the wakes of this youth who has appropriated many new traits
One after the other, memories leave their footprints
From the day he turned aside, to this day
When he puts his maiden steps into the world.

❖

K GODAVARI SARMA

A Ditty at Dawn

I don't think it's an intelligent bargain
To trade-off Larynx for silence.
The moment my ears are awake to the summer's day
The sweet tweeting birds
Encourage me to become a poet.
Kindling the fire in my gullet
And shutting my mouth
I continue to recline idling on the bed.
Words would be cooking within.

I hate to play a Dussasana
With ideas sleeping cozily like creased ironed clothes,
Dragging them by hair.
I have the patience of a child
Watching eagerly at the tree
Waiting for the guava to ripen.

Suddenly, like the song of Saigal
On air on the Radio,
An image silently blossoms in my mind.
Shaking off my sleepy-bedsheet
I sit up
To become a Poet.

◆

AFSAR

An Erasion

The shore
Is a nest built by the sea
Diligently collecting each grain of sand.

And the day inevitably dawns sometime
When
You have to erase
Not only your shore...
But even your sea

You can't help it.

For a Catharsis

Yes
One has to write
At least to apprehend the quietude
After a prolonged battle.
To assert that man is a tree that can blossom
One must write.
Creation is but a translation of the world...
Creation is destruction in the first place...
As one writes
Pen traces plough lines on paper
And the vivacity of life flows from fingers to the letters.
After the writing is completed
The train of sentence whistles off
Hauling bogies of words behind
The sound, however, pervades the surroundings.

One has to write...
Write a letter to the world
Answering the Why's and What's...
For a synthesis...
For the sake of a catharsis.
One can write on the sky
Write on the ocean
But
Letters can't be written on the sky
Letter won't retain on the sea
Therefore

One must write about an idea as expansive as the sky
Write about indigence as deep as the sea

Yes, write
That centuries of harassment
Could not shake the confidence about life,
And
That the drops of sweat on the forehead
Efface the writing over there.
And when you write, write
Not on cisterns but on cataracts
Not on leaves but on lives.
Yes, write... and write... and write
Write only in words that shall never dry up.
And the eyes that read them
Should absorb the moisture and moisten

One must write... Yes write
And go on writing for life
Till that timeless sentence suddenly strikes.
And in that enduring writing,
Heart should wear down.

Writing and smearing sandal paste are not the same.
Nobody can stamp out the sense of writing.

❖

Mythical Beauty

I just can't imagine the world without you!
Before you
This world was merely
A place dotted with deserts and saline seas.
When you walked down...
Life sprang to life, and
In your wakes followed greenery,
Rain and a whiff of fresh air.
For that matter
Wasn't it you that brought this day-night cycle?
You are that ecstatic beauty
That cannot be caught
In the web of life and death... Infinitum
Whenever you bless me with a smile
I win as bonus one more life
And I travel along the paths
Of clouds and starry space
Singing praises of you.
Be that you possess a rare physical form
But you seem to linger
On the bourns of mythical shores.
That will-o-the-wisp
The tintinnabulations of your swaying anklet-bells
Send messages
Unintelligible to everybody, but the soul!

◆

SHAJAHANA

The Guest

I said, "Welcome to my guest."
He said, "No, I am a refugee.
A dove that has escaped
The talons of pursuing hawks. "

I just treated him as a guest.
I could not make out what to serve him.

"May I know what would you like...?" I meant food.
"Like taking food with my family," he replied.
He was like a deep dried up well
Hard to peep into.

"Is this something I can safely eat?"
His alarmed looks seem to betray his fears.
"I smell smoke from somewhere," he said.
Ploughing his fingers through the food,
Thinking of his family with every grain he took in...
He did not really seem to relish it...
It was as if he was lifting up with a picotta
His oceanic-grief from abysses within.

He was seemingly here
But was roaming elsewhere.
Thinking of his still untraceable brother,
His kidnapped sister, dismantled families...

Translated from Telugu ● *NS Murty*   **167**

His forced exile from his land... dreaming
Of his ravaged streets, dissipated friend-scape,
Razed down villages and scattered community...
He looked grieving with his whole body
Finding his two eyes inadequate.
And ultimately,
Leaving as silently as he had come, he said:
"Thirsting for blood is a fatal infection."

◆

K GEETA

A Weapon for Thousand Tumours

Death is a charter on stone
Connate with life, the place is predetermined.
One has to submit to it without demur.
Death is a stigma that sticks through life;
And shadows life without ever being erased.
Life hangs on to death
Like a drop of dew to a leaf's apex.
Yet, life is nobler than death
And one has to fight unto the last moment.

O dear body! Don't wail!
A grim silent war wages within, you are unaware
A tumor silently crept into the cells.
Death might be on the wings like a kite
Or, ready to pounce like a cheetah in the thicket,
But, you kindle life... back to fire.

O dear body! Don't grieve.
Don't dab in tears the swelling emotions within.
Don't make me crazy crying for corporal beauty
Instead of comeliness of life.

Yet, my darling! This is a vain affliction.
Will there be a surrogate body sleeping where I was?
Will another frame adorn my attire and ornaments?
And in your warm hands that seize me, will there be...?
Oh! What silly noxious thorny thoughts fill my mind?

*Translated from Telugu * NS Murty*   **169**

Smarting me sharper than reality,
Whichever way I turn in my bed!
No. No. I am not dead.
It's more a fear for treatment, than fear for life.

Darling! What can I say?
The bosom that hugged you dearly each day
Might be missing, but not the heart behind;
When children feel for the cuddle
Your fatherly bosom stands in for mine;
In the trail of chemo's and radiations
Whatever happened within,
Hair dropped down like powder, without.
Yet my loveliness...
The loveliness of my heart did not cease.
I did not decease as yet.
Forget about the beauty...
Every time the body resisted
It threw up guts with vengeance.

Darling! Pray! Save me!
Show me an easier and better alternative.
The thoughts that swing like a pendulum to and fro
Are scarier than nightmares.
Is there no exception for virtuoso artists?
Won't the days when I ruled the roost return?
Behind that visual beauty
There lies that dream-eating Cancer worm
There was something wrong somewhere
The baby is yet to learn babbling
And the eldest son is hardly ten

O, God! Please don't curse my children.
Don't alienate for the greenhorns
Their mother from them

Don't leave this body with a pain,
More painful than death itself.

No. No.
There is no room for fear.
In this life of Snakes and Ladders,
How can we afford not repairing the impaired steps?
How long can we go on wailing vainly
As if we were afflicted with a weeping sickness?
Even if our moments are numbered,
How can we live dying each moment,
Until we actually do?

My beloved body!
Come on! Blossom!
Fill those cells with spirit and eyes with confidence
Be the weapon
That doesn't give a hoot to thousand tumors.
Beat the drum of life
Sending shivers across the decrees of death.

(To the victims of Breast Cancer)

❖

KAVI YAKOOB

Snare

It has been long since soil lost faith in man.

In an age when one sees no grain but only ensnaring nets,
Poor birds, they still land on land in hope.
Another season has been added afresh now
To the list of seasons,
To take seize of the birds and the grain.

Innocent farmer!
He never knew any fable,
Other than the birds flying away with the net.
To this new huntsman, however,
Grain has been dearer than the farmer.

Farmer is a synonym for pledging and pawning.

When the familiar
"Harrows"
And "funnels of a drill plough"
Disappear from the tongue,
And unfamiliar terms and unheard relations
Become tools,
The canopy looks bewildering!
With accursed future,
Hybridized seeds,
And hissing machinery,
The backbone of this country

Has now reduced to
A lone hapless wooden mast ravaged by termites.

As human relations get washed in dollars,
The farmer is weaned away from Nature,
To lean on her stead, the machine.

In her own interest,
And no longer trusting the nets
That snare man,
Soil
And the Nature,
Time heralds:
The Earth needs freedom!

A Dash of Exquisite Beauty

Hemmed between the ethereal and the mundane,
Gasping for breath in the apartments,
Wandering through the currents of civilization like an ant-head,
For once, one evening,
Looking at the scintillating browny sun on the occidental sky
I slipped into my cherished memories' album.

On the meadow canvas of my mind
One memory, still green, shakes off
And takes off like a kite...
Hovering over the known and unknown terrain, exhausted,
Settles ultimately on a string of impressive experiences.

Sitting me on the bed of branches, rollicking,
Bathes me in showers of nectar of soft, delicate flowers.
The wing touches me ever so gently
And sneaking under my eyelids
Leaves me in a world of magical realism.

My childhood
Which capered around my village like a belled calf,
Becomes a sugar lump near the Basil plant this moment,
And on the next moment becomes
A salivating holy Sagittarian-month's offering on a banana leaf.
For a while moments of my dabbling with the classics
Appear a fresh leaving indent on my memory.

As if sieged by my childhood pals
I enter my village, choked with emotion
In a new frame of mind.
Velvet green fanning branches,
Pageants of birds doing aerobatics,
The sly-eyed watery ways,
The dense lotus pond,
And gold-panicled rice fields...

Like a ripple, nay, an eternal stream, they stay within me.
Whenever my village comes to my mind
I forget myself... recalling her exquisite beauty.

❖

VINNAKOTA RAVISANKAR

A Wintry Dawn

Bright is the sunshine
Yet, there is little warmth in it.
It seems even the Sun
Shivers under the cold.

The pleasure of seeing the night off
Doesn't last a wee longer.
The day looks as if the sorceress Cold
Has only donned new attire for a change.

The sky waits yearningly
For the rare shadow of a bird

And the tree
Which had not shed its leaves
Drags its own shadow rather heavily.

An unknown fear seizes time and again
And the cold wind of memories
Nips through, occasionally.

One feels like folding himself up into his own self,
Shrinking back,
To undo evolution of this lone body
Into the confines of that single primal cell.

◆

VIMALA

A Silent Hymn

Ambient silence after the cremation of a corpse.
A terrible silence
On every wood, knoll, and cottage
Even on people in the end
A pall of silence settles.
When you look at it
You get goosebumps
Recalling a pacific-looking sea.
You can't bear such unnerving silence…
A silence where your heartbeat is so audible to you!
You shoot a question

But,
There is silence in answer...
There
The door panel hollowed by the tearing bullet
A plant sheared of a length of its bark
A damp undried strain of blood on the road
None of them may be intelligible to you, but
The sound on the lips silenced by
The din of the striped devil hovering overhead
And the streak of sanguine in the staring eyes
Must have surely answered you.
Silence is the grief
That rolls through the eyes piercing the heart.
A silence ...so inhuman.

Translated from Telugu ● *NS Murty*   **177**

The wounds on the branches inflicted by the metallic boots
Hurt you deeply at heart.
It's abominable to bear the bestiality
That sucks the human blood like a blotting paper!
Stillness... is still the answer.

Yet...
The shouts of "Fire, Fire"
Echo in the air across the sky still.
And the half-erased haphazard fleeing footprints stay.
All these may be unintelligible to you, but
The silent fist of the Gond raised
After feeling the wet, bloodied bandage
Must have surely answered you

The silent currents of the sea
Are readying for a war.
It is the ominous silence of the sea
Before the waves surge into tides
The silence
Between the hands raised to beat the tom-tom
And the beat
Stays
But for a fraction of a second.

◆

NARAYANASWAMY VENKATAYOGI

Three Cheers to Life!

Lads!
This is your granny appealing
With folded hands
I swear upon me
Please don't part with yourselves
For nothing.

There are no more tears left
And I am frail, can't even wail bitterly;

I am unable to stand
When you turn lifeless before my very eyes
Instead of becoming mighty spears;

My heart rends
When children afire like live coals
Reduce to cinders at the fireplace;

Will you leave me destitute
Who nursed you to the last drop
Of my dried up breast?

Before bashing the beast
That enslaved us?

Lads!
Tell me, why you should die,
While people taking others' lives
Shamelessly roam around?
Callow youth like tender teak-leaves,

Translated from Telugu ● *NS Murty*

Why should you wither and dry up first?
Green horns like the young mangoes
Why should you drop down?
Like the glitter on the waters
Why should you disappear?

Children!
Don't lose heart!
Don't lose faith on life!
Plant your feet firm on the ground!

Feel the spirit of these throbbing veins
On my hands.
Remember the anger of our people
Who fought with guns and won.

Children!
Why do you waste away
Your youthful vigor?
And put out with waters of death
Your fiery anger of a burning kiln?

These ropes are twined
Not to work as noose around your neck,
But to bind and bang the wild elephants
That have been trampling us all the while.
The kerosene cans are not meant
For you to douse and take lives,
But to burn those bastards in public
Who have robbed us of all that we have.

Come on! Children!
Let's unite and stay together.
Clap together and raise our voice
Let's give three cheers to life
That the earth and heaven reverberate with:
"The Future is ours."

❖

ANISETTI RAJITA

'Mother' is not Singular

It's the mother earth, overflowing with oceans,
That has breathed the idea of love at epochal time,
And still, replicates life in every inch of this creation.
She is an eternal spring that embraces all waters.
Mother is a ceaseless source of monumental love
She is the beauty incarnate
And, the survival of humanity solely rests on her.
If one can still breathe and life beats, it is thanks to
Her varietal roles and intellectual essence.
It is because of this wonderful mother
Sun rises or sinks each day.
If the wheel of seasons rolls down
Or, limits of time are expand;
If the deciduous trees dress themselves up
With delicate shoots flaunting daintiness of spring;
If the cuckoos continue to coo
And we could witness full- and new-moons
It's courtesy omnipresence of mother only.
A mother is not a mother to only one, or to only few;
A mother is not just a lone and singular being,
Mother means many, mother is collective.
She is the primal natural force
That set this universe into motion
She is a manifestation of humanity itself.
Mother is not singular, but plural
She is a veritable definition of plurality.

❖

Translated from Telugu ◈ *NS Murty*

After Bidding Adieu

She walks silently across the bridge
As if she has caressed a flower with her delicate hands;
Or, feathered a branch along her rosy cheeks.

The bridge, like man, whelms in spring
Becoming a flower
And a greenish sprig.

After she crosses the bridge over
She looks back for a brief moment
And then swiftly marches ahead... her own way.

Enveloping that look around him like a rainbow
And gathering colorful skies around
Wishing it were the end of his life
The bridge stands alone... resolutely.

SIKHAMANI

House of Yellow Curtains

One summer morning
When day was breaking on the orient
I visited a house draped with yellow curtains
Overlooking the garden, over that towering knoll.

No sooner had I stepped in I felt
It must be the very house, Peddana was talking about:
A secret... silent ... secluded ... spot.
Cool white marble under feet, and
White-faced whitened walls
With windows open on all the four sides.
While the curtains screened off the baby sun rays
A light orange glow filled and coated the interior.
And in one corner, on the tripod over the black earthen pot
Green creepers in Fevicril stretch their tendrils.
The plumes of peacock in the pot
Nod their heads for a feathery whiff of air.
Garlands of speechless red and green parrots
Adorn either side of the door.
A fine jingle of hanging bells touched by gentle breeze is audible
Like the secret whispering of sweet nothings by a mistress.
Perhaps some poet who finished a great poem in trance
Might just have gone in, leaving his pen on paper.
The cane chair he has rocked in up till now

Is still rocking as if someone is swinging it, and
Like a good poem that rocks a discerning reader.

❖

KONDEPUDI NIRMALA

I Take Risk

First peg...

I take risk when my man is with the bottle
When I hit the road to get oil for the evening bread
He reaches home with a full bottle.
My wisdom tooth smarts... hinting what's up...
Peeping in for 'Soda' he shoots a happy laugh
Intimate honeymoon photo on the wall
Watches on in bewilderment...
Setting everything up elaborately with religious fervor
He opens up the cork with great indulgence
Effervescence kick-starts emptying into the glass
Cheering into the vacuum he pours down a gulp
Of course, he would never forget cheering even if he
Were in great hurry.
I worry looking for ways to screen him off from children.
A word into this ear doesn't reach the other
For, Johnny Walker blocks the two.
'By the way,' he asks,
'Does the new pair of chappals pinch you still?'
'Can't help even if it does; I live-in with it,' I answer.

Second peg...

When my bunny is with the bottle I take risk...
He reaches out for the second peg leaning forward
I change the channel to a horror movie in the TV to

Set right the wailing children fighting with each other
Measuring scales, abandoning homework.
The three stay put there... stunned.
'I don't want this mess at my home.' I throw away the ladle
'It's not your home, mine,' he shuts the door hard on my face
"F**k your mother, f**k your sister..." swearing begins...
Volleys of taboos from one end go unheard at the other
For, there lies the same haughtiness
On both tongues peppered by the same salt.
Without any fault of theirs, poor parents and sisters of both,
Stand devoid of character in their places
Honeymoon photo in close embrace, clings to the wall in fright.

Third peg...

The house dozes in sleep...
I peep in to check whether he is in or out
Like a slivered 'Chili Bajji' my love-of-life reels on the floor.
Patting him on his shoulder, I call him up for dinner
'You...! What an arrogance! You liken husband to chappals?'
He raises his hand...
I wrench the same hand and whack it to the wall behind.
This hit doesn't care that hit

Fourth peg...

Though my eyes take to sleep, my body keeps awake
'What arrogance! You make your husband bite chappals?'
The devil in the bottle grumbles still. And
Grumbling for a while more, he vomits his stomach out.
His character comes out in translucent spells.
And the pajama gets drenched in the government liquor

When my man is with the bottle, I take risk.
I throw on his head the bucketful of water kept in readiness
Johnny Walker from this side and government liquor from that side

Go down the drain jostling each other
This drain doesn't hear what that drain says
For, the same dross of a minister's promise floats over them both.
The bear hugging honeymoon couple
Part ways abruptly and elope with their mates

When my man is with the bottle, I take great risk.

❖

K GEETA

A Plot of Mushrooms

A filament of white hair flashes on my forehead
Rather disconcertingly.
Like a ripened leaf
Grazing against the branch,
Like, say, for the first time
The merciless Fall setting in rather too early,
Somewhere within me reverberate
The cracking sounds of aged dry branches.

A new pain aches sitting heavy on the head
At the thought of the year turning new.
Strange!
The childhood yearning of growing big soon
Grows like wart now under eyes, against will.
I can't recall to have cast
The seeds of age on my cheeks.
Are these the very lofty shoulders
That coolly bore the melting age once
Without a flinch?
What a pity! They are earth-bound now!

What a time childhood was!
There were no masks.
No fears.
Nor worries about the upcoming years.
Like these days
One never saw somebody else in the reflection

Standing before the mirror;
Nor had to be conscious about his crown.

The second half of life
Had become a white thorn pricking over head.
Know not what it feeds on, but
It twins up overnight
However carefully the weed is pruned
And had reduced to a plot of mushrooms
By the end of the year.
The forehead had become a desert of undulating sand dunes.

Oh! I must be crazy.
Can a yacht travel back in a gushing stream?
Can the head fail to ripe because the mind did not?

How nice it would be
If there are dyes for the mind like we have for head!
As time approaches
Doubling up to devour
We need some new life prisms now
To disperse whiteness into colorful spectra.
We need brand new spectacles
That can see both sides of the coin.

KOPPARTHY

A Nightmare

Morning
When the door is opened
A whiff of cool breeze nips

As the eyes search for newspaper
They find little shoes
Left forgotten to keep them inside
The night before

A subtle thought...
That the little darling child
Who used to wear them always
Might be standing there all night
Keeping her feet within
Joins the cool wind
To nip.

◆

ADURI SATYAVATHI DEVI

A Corf of Chalk

Caught in the chilling web of sagittal month
Time shivers in the bitter biting cold.
Even in the congested cities
The foreyards of houses take a head bath
And get cleansed off their inured dirt.
And before dawn
In chalky designs they get adorned
As if milky ways were spread out,
A swarm of swans were floating away,
And seem a queen's entourage
Has been sojourning in that floral palanquin.

There in that remote corner of the village
A leftover place after the city had engulfed very inch in its reach
On that half-quarried hillock
A hunch-backed old hag, looking like a hackneyed moon,
Sapped of all energies
Labors in the pit in front
Herself... becoming a fistful of hunger.

She anneals her bones bitten by cold with the rays of the sun
And becomes a machine to grind the hill to dust.
Filling up her basket with her labour
And bearing her life-support overhead,
She marches past the six-bus stops distance for three hours
Measuring distances in her accustomed way
Of the amount of sweat she perspires.

She bargains her appetite with the city dwellers
For a hunk of bread and few drops of tea
And satiates her hunger.

Positing the change in the navel
She retires for a nap under some wayside tree
Or some shade under the sun.
Reminiscing her experiences as ripe as her chalky head,
Between those half asleep eyelids she shivers all of a sudden
Fearing her fate if the city were to snatch
Even those remains of the hillock.

When it happens, won't the foreyards of houses pale away
Devoid of chalky designs
Like a queen divested of her decorations?

◆

SIVA REDDY

Mother

What do I know about being a mother, after all!
I can never be a mother myself!

I never knew what it's like being fertile
Or how to glean the essence
From all soils and infuse life into it.

I never knew how to collect imaginings from
All directions and planetary systems,
From the clusters of starry skies,
From endless oceanic expanses, from whiffs of air,
From leaves, flowers, tufts of grass,
From surging waters within and without
From deers, peacocks,
And birds that suddenly swoop and surface over waters
To catch sun between their beaks
And give it to a being.

I never know how to catch the purple reflections
Of 'Light of life' beaming from every twig,
And grace it to life

I never knew to separate sleep from night,
Wakefulness from day,
Hunger from the rosy mouths of birdlings in the nest
And give to the life wobbling in the womb

Translated from Telugu ● *NS Murty*   **193**

I never knew to sit, as if sitting for ages,
And to look searchingly at all nooks of the universe
To pick up something beyond my imagination and reach
And present it to a child.

I never knew to deftly pick up the solitude of the isles
Beauty from the bodies, gleam of the green seminal beds,
And the skill of small birds that walk on waters with ease
And give them to a dreaming boy

And unlike the lady in the Neruda's poem
Who stood stoically alone amidst ambient devastation,
I don't know how to wait... and wait... and wait
To stand and stand and stand, and give a measure to the child
To measure the lengths of waiting looks.
What do I know about being a mother, after all!
I cannot be a mother myself!

But if I can't be a mother even when I hold the pen,
How can these letters come to life?
Come of age? And fledge and fly?

❖

VADREVU CHINAVEERABHADRUDU

An Afternoon in Agra

That was an afternoon in Agra.

As the late Sagittal sun
Prevailed up the welkin,
Like the tang of a tarty fruit,
There was a mild bite in it.

That ageless dream... Taj Mahal... looked as if
Somebody had set it over this earth only yesterday.

The marmoreal Minars were
Splendid under the hoary afternoon sun.
Another generation of admirers
Lie in front of it... spellbound.

In the lawn in front of me there was a flower
And a Bumble Bee was hovering over its antheral centre.
The bee for the flower
And the flower for the bee.
My eyes were feasting on
The essay of their meetings and partings.

Endlessly... people were flocking around
The delectable monument with cameras in hand.

There was an invincible flower
In front of me that afternoon.
That might have withered by the end of the day.
But the Bumble Bee there, was
Tipsier with love than Shah Jahan.

❖

An Earthen Pot

Someone is walking away
Sacking the clay
Sedimented
On the banks
Abraded and
Shoved by Time.

Wetting the heap of argil
On the potter's wheel occasionally,
The Moment is
Pressing it to shape.

Separating it from the wheel in a trice
Like a midwife who snaps the umbilical,
Youth harmonizes it
Tapping it with a spatula.

Manhood is the brittle,
Shapely, unburnt pot
Dried up in the sun.
It is time to burn it
In the kiln of life.

Sir!
Putting your ears to it
And tapping it with your knuckles
You test my quality.
Am I sound?

O, my dear son!
You circle around the pyre
With potful of water
Without looking back.
Child!
Hold the pot rather carefully!

NISHIGANDHA

A Moist Memory

Listening to the affairs of changing Seasons
Thawing ice leaves its last wet traces.
A memory stops me on a chilly night
Holding me by my little finger.
What is night, after all?
Just disappearance of your voice!
I still light each of my days
With your last greeting heard decades back.
Bowers of reconciliation
Surround the ebony hole around the heart.
Sprinkling handfuls of waters of hope
Every now and then is inevitable!
When the few jasmines of affection hold up
The absent-minded west wind on a moony night,
Old memories of caressing... shower around.
The cadence of the pigeon turning restlessly
On the other side in its sleep,
Retraced the imprints of your lips on my eyelids.
The springs of tears that suddenly swelled up in my eyes
Soaking up the inertial Time say:
In this world of your absence
Well, it might be possible to live,
But, it's not that easy!!!

◆

NANDAKISHORE

Everything is Obvious

1

It is not possible for her.
And, it is beyond me.
There is no gain blaming each other.

2

Nobody would agree for us.
Her people's houses are secure under lock and key,
Mine is an open sky where sun visits at will.

3

It is just the same always.
Youth and life are not one and the same.
Whatever comes can't remain forever; even if it were she.
Visiting is something; staying behind is another.

4

However much I try, the wailing won't cease.
On the eclipsed hands, even moon doesn't shine
And the wound won't heal where there is no oxygen.

5

Tell me! What will you do
When people petrify in your very presence?
When God himself hangs bat-like,
Who else could reassure?

Translated from Telugu ● *NS Murty*

When somebody's looks torture you,
And the heart prays for a body;
When someone's words scissor you
And the body seeks for a sacrifice;
Where will you immolate?
On what starry altar shall you annihilate yourself?

◆

MOHANTULASI RAMINENI

Do You Know?

Do you know that a tear had been shed for you?
Do you know that a grapheme had spilt over?

No matter whatever you know,
Things just go their wonted way.

The Coral Jasmine in the backyard
Continue to rain in heaps;
When I look at the nascent purity and intensity of
Their red and white
I feel the truth of your existence under the blue skies.

God! How many words
The migrant bird might be concealing under its wing!
Perhaps to appropriate a new shade of freedom
From every place it migrates to.
Otherwise, how could the wings span so wide?
How dearly I wish
It lends them to my thoughts for a while!!

The parting day
Fails to devour the twinkling lamps.
Even this blackholish path
Is unable to swallow the sporadic vehicular beams.

After watching your sweet smile in the full moon
All sensuous hearts
Twinkle... soused in pleasure.

❖

I Don't Know Why

I don't know why...

Not that there wasn't any pain,
Only that it doesn't precipitate into tears.

Grief besieges... no doubt,
But it is not possible to wail the heart out.

Yes, I can perceive the frangible heart breaking
But I can't put up a gloomy face.

We cannot speak out certain things
We can't express some others
If a cloud about to burst refrains on second thoughts
We can't blame that her love for the land had evaporated.

I can't answer every damn allegation...
I can't subscribe to the resolution
That one has to take sides to live.

Not that I don't have love for you,
But it's beyond me to prove it is green, at every turn

◆

MANASA CHAMARTI

A Shooting Star

If he were a jungle
She wanted to nestle in his heart like a jingle of verdure

If he were a sea
She wanted to dissolve like a drop of rain in his expanse

Had he teased her like the sky
She wanted to give a peck on his cheek like a star.

He was only
A fleeting spring
And a teeming stream.

Had he been the firmament
She wouldn't have plummeted like a shooting star, perhaps!

❖

SRINIVAS VASUDEV

Confessions

1

I came walking over the night
But could not collect a fistful of darkness!
The dreams behind the eyes swimming in tears
Could not make a legend.

2

Sitting in each grapheme
I converse with the rest.
For, each word is a confession-box.
I put down my own episodes here.

3

Like the empty bottles rolling down
These memories trudge along encasing emptiness.
Some never get interred,
While some others get hazy
Like inky letters on a dampened paper.

4

Some enigmatic relations restrain emotions
Like the weight on a paper.
Passion had long evaporated!
When shall the distinction between
Dampening and moistening be clear?

5

The howling in the air
That the interred had no friends
Shall not reach the other ear.
No boulder of the Pyramids
Can either fill the hollowness of life
Or block my view.
But then, what is it that I attempt to see,
After all!

6

Borrowed intellect shall not fit
Like the misfitting borrowed garments
It looks so odd... so out of place.

7

That all-pervading vacuum
Does not spare even this confession box.
Doesn't Life script its own screen play?

❖

Translated from Telugu ● *NS Murty*

Darkness and Silence

As if you are imprisoned
Do walls grow around you?
Well, does it matter when you aren't alone
And you don't step forward towards light?
Darkness is the only comrade,
Silence shivers at the slightest tremor
A drama goes behind the veiled curtain,
And all the characters sing the same tune.
From the cracks of the window
Light sneaks-in surreptitiously like a thief.
Having had to live with an adamant lizard
Was the cursed fate of the winged insect.
On the door ajar,
Lie the finger prints of the unknown
Even on the life of unrealized dreams
Runs the writ of anonymous wills.
Darkness gets familiar with speech,
Stillness appreciates the angst; and,
When the un-ceding lamps knock at the door,
Silence recedes to far off shores.

RADHIKA

Bruised Convictions

When
All that I prided over as mine own once
Stares at me like a stranger
And questions my identity;

When
Those exciting moments and sweet memories
I regaled in recollecting over and over
Jeer at me calling me crazy;

I stand on the familiar ground as an alien
Cherishing the wakes of my past within.

This instant
All treasured memories are dashed all of a sudden
And all convictions have reduced to mere fancies.

Enduring Search

Yesterday... and today...
Day in and day out... and,
For eons...
I have been on the search...

What is it that I am seeking after?
Who am I searching for?
What are the places I am looking about?
But,
Why should I search for, at all?
I don't know!
It is an infinitum of questions...
With no definite answers.

Did I ever allow something
To slip through my hands anywhere?
I don't think so.
But yet, I search for that elusive thing
With the illusion that I own it.

Time is fleeting... days are thawing.
Hopes are vanishing... faith is retreating
Life is ceasing... and the spirit depleting
Yet, that crazy search continues...
Cutting through the dense deep darknesses...
To the limits of horizon and to the depths of oceans
For that evanescent enigmatic something.

Till breath snaps
Till spirit saps
My being becomes ethereal...
Maybe,
This search shall endure... ever... forever!

PRASUNA RAVINDRAN

Today

Silent is the wee-hour mist, and
Chime melodiously the temple-bells...
Enough!
This heart is awake.

Be as it may
The page of the day
Blacken for any pollutant...

But,
Before the darkness of the night
Could thicken deep,
It would turn out pleasant
Like a moon-washed poem.

◆

Darling Daughter

Before the tailless squirrels
And nameless flowers
Join the unfinished drawings,
Colours engage in whispers
With the walls and the windows.

When that exhausted and disheveled rainbow
Wakes up from her sound sleep
It strikes dawn in the mansion.
All the curtains of inertia will be
Drawn aside in a hurry.

As the notes are dunked in milk
In an attempt to attune them
Playmate parrots
Touch down gently beside.
A garden blooms amidst the four walls of the room.

With the taction of nascent leafy runs
And the lays of cooing laughter
Spring flourishes through
The mornings.

Celebrating the favorite festival
In the bubbling laughter of collecting tads of paper
Declaring an uncalled for breather all of sudden
No sooner she locks my knees with her tender hands...

Translated from Telugu ● *NS Murty*   **211**

There springs in my eyes anew
A green memory of mother's moist hand
When she kissed tweaking my cheek
Stopping her work in the middle
Long long ago.

◆

MAHESHKUMAR KATHI

I

The wink that lies between two successive breaths...
The note that complements a harmony by its omission...
The word which elevates a poet's fancy to a poem by its elision
The ideation perceived before it turns into a thought...
The vacuous horizon where the elements meet...

I am
That wink...
That note...
That word...
That idea...
And
That vacuum.

VAMSIDHAR REDDY

Apparition

When I was returning home from a late night show
I saw the person,
Supposed to have been dead twenty days back,
Smoking a cigarette gracefully.

No doubt about that. He was the very person.
I attended his obsequies and dined in their house.
Pity, he should frighten me when I was all alone!

Noticing his feet were not turned behind,
I dared putting my foot forward.
He seems to have guessed what I was about to ask.
"Sir! Please don't speak about this to anybody.
I am deep in debts.
I just played this trick for the insurance money.
When I get the money, I shall repay you too
And we move away from this place."

Six months passed.

I went to his house when I was hard pressed for money.
I mooted about the insurance money during conversation.
His wife said,
"Brother! He never had any insurance policy."

From then on, I never went to a late night show.

◆

KATTA SRINIVAS

Sitting on the Edge

One midnight hour
I would be reading my own poems
Flipping through the pages of my old diaries
And amuse at the amateur expressions.
Striking off those lines mercilessly...
And before tearing off the pages on the spur
I refrain
As I wish to see them through the eyes of my admirers.
I carefully dress the pages off their folds
And digging deep into the expressions I strike off
I become a Paleologist
And an Archaeologist for a while.
Till another midnight
They sit heavy in my mind.

Android

I need some pain.
A pain that can squeeze my heart dry.
Honestly! There is no catch here,
Nor an ounce of exaggeration.
For,
Somehow, I became immune and turned mechanical
And an exile from myself.
There are no longer any sleepless nights,
Haunting memories, or, burning passions.
Nor have I the faith that I can love truly and dispassionately.

For that matter,
I don't have even a clear cognizable existence.
I want some truth,
A truth that can liberate me from hypocritical lies.

It should be like
The sun that can filter into the AC rooms;
And a hunger
That only poverty can burn within.

I need
Two drops of unsimulated tears;
A wound that time can't heal;
And, a night that can see no dawn.

I need some of that 'earlier me' for myself.
Yes, I need some of that 'me' for myself...

A way... to get out of this inertia...
No longer the Ghazals are able to wet my eye
No longer the revolutions produce horripilations in me
No longer my heart yearns for loneliness
And more importantly,
I don't feel that want... needed for a poem.

I know...
The body degenerates with time.
But I am more afraid, if my soul would as well.

There is something wrong with evolution somewhere.
For,
Maturity fails to prick me for this mediocrity.
I need to die.
Pray, somebody please bury me.
I need to be born again
To reclaim the thing that I have lost
And must hug it dearly with all my heart.

There is no longer any pleasure in the comforts,
And grief fails to produce any grieving in me.
It must have been ages
When I had last wailed my heart out!
Perhaps,
The seas under these eyelids have dried up to deserts.

❖

MOHANATULASI   RAMINENI

Just Let This Night Pass

Just let this night pass...
Spring shall dawn with the daybreak!

Look over there, the last tree on the turn,
Shall start budding and the Cuckoo shall coo
Through the morning window;
Shedding its inhibitions
The Mango shall bloom all over its dense foliage;
To the Sun climbing over the orient
Roof top shall dab humid vapors.
And all the buried wakes shall yield scents of memories.

Just let this night pass...
Spring shall dawn with the daybreak!
The petticoat of childhood
Shall flutter in the lukewarm breeze
And the nest of memories on the Guava of the backyard
Shall think of me once more.
The name that was secretly written and erased
In the crimson vesper hours
Shall visit as a leisurely cloud and water the spirits.
And soon... the festival with the smack of
Fresh jute packing twine shall follow.

Just let this night pass...
Spring shall dawn with the daybreak!
Moments glad and grief that passed

By turns, shall watch over the autumnal night;
The clock that has seen many seasons turn over
Longs for just one lasting memory;
And the jasmine bud peeps into the last drop of dew
Hanging by the awning for her reflection.

Just let this night pass...
Every receding wave of the ocean
Shall surge forth dredging beautiful shells in its fold.

Just let this night pass...
By day... he will be here!

SAIF ALI GOREY SYED

Ghalib!

Ghalib!

Oceans continue to have high and low tides still
Carpenter Bees continue to hover over flowers
The sky continues to play chameleon at will
Plants still sprout only after the seed explodes...

Ghalib!

Darkness still puts on that ebony mantle, and for that
The glow-worms lay in wait for the whole day;
No matter how high-rise the building is,
The gentle breeze continues amusing itself with window leaves
Scepters of monarchy no longer exist there
But the specter of the wretched indigence continues to reign.

Ghalib!

The world continues to regale in your poems
Yet, the inevitable continue to betide lives
Every wall continues to get drenched in rain
And some remedy or the other is available for cold

Ghalib!

The inheritance of your wounds continues to prevail
And on the twigs of roses, prickles continue to shoot,
And entwining brambles, the blooming creepers still survive.
It's only you that is missing, that's all! People haven't changed
And even the Moon continues to exhibit the same old phases

Ghalib!

The cook continues to have the first taste of dish
And only the farmer harvests the crops still,
Religion continues to have good currency
And the watch continues to turn its hands.

Ghalib!

Everything comes out of nothing
And for nothing everything ceases
Darkness continues to lay siege of the lamp
And from somewhere, a cuckoo empties its strains.

Ghalib!

Beautiful Cups of wine are churned out continuously
And the garlands of jasmine girdled amidst others
Continue to wither along with others by daybreak

Ghalib!

Even when the front seats are vacant
People still prefer to stand back
To listen to your poetry rendering
And they continue to search for
What you had searched before.
Yet, they couldn't find the veritable truth.

Ghalib!

Darkness to light
And light into darkness continue to transform
The lone man continues to be alone
And in the absence of eupnoea
Bodies turn to termite colonies.

❖

NANDA KISHORE

How Can I be a Poet?

Do you know?
I love. I love her, the very idea of her,
And every inch of her ...always and endlessly
I love...
With nothing else to do or say
I just go on loving her.
The whole village would be wailing either
For the crop being dry, or field becoming fallow;
For the loss of grain to rain, or to sudden sweeping flood;
For the crop being lost to the pests, or to the beasts; or
For want of money to pay the principal, or the interest
...ad infinitum.
And it migrates in search of a greener pastures.

Not lagging behind, I too migrate into my thoughts...
Bear-hug her and get lost in the thoughts
Of the moments I spent in her presence;
About our love-making, about the past memories
Or the enduring ignorance; I try to recollect them most
And scribble a semblance of poetry.

From dawn to dusk the whole village breaks its neck
And the sweat streams down to wet the verdurous fields
I too assay in my imaginings showering springs of fond desires.
I liken the spectrum to her varied hues
And regale it is all a manifestation of my love.

Due either to inefficient administration or corruption
Prices go northwards and the quantities southwards.
Feet find it hard to drag themselves.
Oblivious to the pervading suffering
I continue my flights into her imagination
I will be lavish of my words but miserly in my ideas.
Strange, it never hurts or embarrasses me
When I had to buy water in cans
Unable to find a draught in the open;
Or when I had to walk down miles
For the kiss of a fresh breeze...
They never spur me to write a poem.
Skyscrapers appropriate the sky before my very eyes
They steal the Sun and hide the Moon behind,
I recreate the clouds and the skies in my mind
And shall hover between the cellar and the penthouse
And in that invisible vacuous loneliness
I still want not words in praise of her beauty
That the moonlight is her countenance or
Light ... a reflection of her smiles...
Some such crazy things I write
And drop down stretching my hands skywards.

One or two of my kin join the revolution
And ask me join and lend them a hand.
Answerless, I remain stone dead silent
Occupied with strange and exotic thoughts.
In no time, her memories inebriate me once more.
Death of an activist reaches my ear somehow.
I grieve perfunctorily, and look into the sky.
But, even there, I see her form.
I find her in the brilliance of the Milky Way.
I shut myself from the sheen of martyrs
With impromptu lenses, lest it should reach my eye.

Translated from Telugu ● *NS Murty*   **223**

Life succumbs to an accident as I watch
People in the hospital wail their eyes and hearts out in agony
I see the handicapped scattered severally but I reach home coolly

The siren of 108* ceases instantly.
Silence envelopes suddenly from nowhere.
I forget everything and reconcile in no time.
I bemoan my endless grief, and pen how deeply she hurt me.
I regale in the bliss of weaving words
And curse myself that I did not get wiser.
I shall be walking everyday amidst the destitute, helpless
The half-clad and the forced prostitutes...
But I turn a Nelson's eye to their nudity

Describing her unseen blooms of youth
And dreaming of hugging her
I doze in the sedation of that poetry.
I revel, besot with her love
Shaking me to my senses
Somebody pleads me to write something
Turning over the pages of newspaper,
I make up for my lack of emotion and
I throw out words dabbed in glycerine-tears
I am averse to rewriting history
Nor even commission my mind to read it
Yet, it seems I know enough...
No matter what people think of me.

With no sense of the present,
I always dream of her every day.
Fall sets about in many families with War
Knives a-flower with every swish
Guns and bombs turn up in their own seasons
Capitalism craves for its prestige.
But I will be steeped in affected naturality to enjoy her spirit

And I will be madly searching for her
Walking through the pools of blood.
Scorning her sometimes and importuning at other times,
Giving form to my imaginary love,
I question her knowing the answers before.
I am unable to make out still,
What for the poet is there after all?
For himself? Or, for the society?

* *108 is a medical, accident relief, police and fire Emergency Service available in many states of India.*

PRAVEENA KOLLI

Endless Saga

Sometimes the day, and
Sometimes the night
I wonder
Where they beget these infirmities from!

As if the land is yeaning,
And the sky were scrimpy
These ideas well up to the brim!
Even as you drain out these memories in oodles
They ooze up in springs … eternally!

How lucky are the cumulonimbi!
They can dump their melancholy
By raining it out.
But what a tragedy!
The gravity of tears
Shall continue to collect, than cease
However much they stream down the eyelids.

Strangely enough,
Some aches and agonies
Shall never surcease.
Even if we illude
That the pain of the wounds has abated,
The throbbing of the memories
Shall remain, oddly, forever green.

The lips of the thawing time
Shall hum the tune of an old lyric eternally...
Till life lasts.
The melody of memory generated
Shall croon within
The aural confines time has excepted.

Every event, every occasion
Is a perplexing move on snakes and ladders!
More than the pleasure of catapults by the ladder
The snakebites of scrutiny
Shall smart longer often.

Every syllable, every imagining
Is an endless saga
Like the fabric on the loom
Short of a weft or a warp always.

MANASA CHAMARTI

On the Shores of Intimacy

That's an age-old picture-freeze
The grin of the froth
At the lukewarm caress on his soaked feet
Stars over his lips.

Leaning over his shoulder and looking into the horizon
She would be drinking with her eyes
The bantering between Sky and the Sea.

The wind and wave play peek-a-boo with the skin;
Shadows play chiaroscuro before eyes;
They trade a host of sweet nothings from their heart
As handfuls of liquid-sand filters through their toes

Before the camphoric sun sank under the sea-line
All his love becomes an oblation offered at her feet
And the exotic hues her restless sari flaunts
Kindle new brilliances in his heart

People who cannot foresee the clusters of light
Darkness can unveil in misgivings through intimacy
Are simply lost in the dialectics of how
The sky and the sea ever really meet at all!

◆

NARAYANA SARMA MALLAVAJJALA

A Book Slipping from Rack

Like aan unexpected call from an old friend
A book slips down from the bookrack.

How many tears he might have shed, the poet,
And how much he must have struggled to gather himself...
He was tenderly humane here and there
And equally arrogant even times,
Sometimes, strong and severe
Like the ever effusive stream of memories.

We do pick up the books randomly from the rack
But do we really care many others that beckon?

If some of them twine us
Like flowers and garlands in a meet, or a meeting;
Some others hug us endearingly
Like our young or old siblings.
What is there in a name
When they fill this hive with sweet nectar?

One book is missing.
I feel the loss of some close friend.
Retiring to my solitude
I shall search for my lost self.

❖

Translated from Telugu ● *NS Murty*   **229**

One Relation and Several Realizations

You have your logic and I have mine own argument
A strange situation of nobody being politically wrong.

The matter of interest is no longer
Who parted from the other first?
And to expect answers for every question
Is nothing short of madness.

We are inured to disappointments expecting high
We can't help but live in whimsical imaginations.
Lugging the weights and counting the miles
We stay put still where we have been.

You travel your way, and I exile my own way.
Tragic moments of no one being wrong.

Now the issue remains
Who remained himself intact?
It's of no consequence now whether
The lessons of life learnt shall rescue or not.

◆

BHASKAR KONDREDDY

Metaphysical

When she is dragged along
The rough gravel and dirt village road
Tying her legs to a rope without concern,
What bitch can offer her teats
To the pitiful pups following their mother?

They were by her side till yesterday
Vying with one another
And rolling playfully one over the other
Teasing and tasting the motherly love
Blissfully sucking her teats at will
Snuggling between her legs.

Poor pups! When the dark wintry night
Frightens them tomorrow with a spell of snow
How could they chase away their worst fears
And find some cosy roof to sleep under coolly?

In the endless catechetical inquiry
Of life after death, no answer is firm or final.
But yet, in walking so along,
Maybe, the grief drives... to soothe itself.

But then,
Why the clear-eyed helpless whelps
That know not shedding tears
Follow their mother?

❖

PRASUNA RAVINDRAN

Things That Matter

SomeSometimes,
It would be just like that!

We would rather imprison
Those butterflies of thoughts
In our heart
Than allow them to float free
Liberating from the sensibilities

Even as the rain water
Collected in the cusps of our hands
Leaks out through the fissures
Between fingers,
The chill and freshness
Of the ethereal skies
Linger still.

If you think
You have wasted your time
Enjoying the pattering rain
And the prominent moonlight...

Well,
You know not what living is, after all!

◆

ELANAAGA

Comity of Notes

Hot footing over sand dunes with whispers
A hum breezes into the heart.
Holding by the little finger it transports you
Thousands of miles hence with her rhythm.
It feasts ears
Lading winds with perfumes,
And paints the innards of the heart with
An exotic amalgam of past lives and ancient glories.
Enraptured by the melody dabbed in grace
The ecstatic soul loses its essence.
The shoots of pleasure sprouting under the sonorous rain
Bid good bye to all misery.
Over the reeds of beats and notes
The door to the heavenly holds opens up.

So long as the spell of the music sustains
Joy leaps up to cloud nine
And hovers over the bowers of heart.
The moment rendering ceases
Pain resurrects
And the body yearns for another daub of melody
As agony mounts to veritable bounds of hell.

Life without music
Is but an inanimate existence.

MARUVAM USHA

On the Sparrow from My Village

You little sparrow!
Ha, I could make you out....you are from my village.
That cute little nose and those elfin feathers... betray you.
But then, when I ask you if you have come alone,
Why are you so insolent, taking off without answering me?
As if you only have those dainty feathers?
Reconciling that you might not have noticed me,
I just crossed your way
But, no. You did not give even a cursory look at me.
I don't know if I had changed with times
Or time had changed me,
You did not recognize me, for sure.

Let me make another try.
Do you remember the other day
When you hurt your nose gory
Pecking at your own image in the mirror?
Can you recall my chasing you jumping on my feet
And catching you in your flight at last?
And when I left you free far off in the open
You teased me by coming home earlier than me?
Did you forget your taunting me once more
Playing with your mates on the posts
At the jasmine garden of Booriyyagaru
When I went there in a silk petticoat to collect a few flowers
On that festive day, salving my feet with saffron
And wearing anklet bells?

Do you remember your roaming around the place
When my granny was telling me stories
Picking all the grits thrown at you by my sister Kamakshi?
Isn't it you who protected the crop
Weeding out the pests in Ramannatata's farm?
This is exactly how you dissed at me last time
When I wanted to check up with you
The lore I heard about you.
Though I left that place you stayed behind.
Maybe, you could not find a mate, like me,
To enchant you out to alien lands.
You were even greeting me
Whenever I came home for festival or vacation.
But suddenly, one day, when my brother Venu said:
"Did you hear, sister? All the sparrows have disappeared suddenly.
They say, they might have been dead?"
I was so sad and depressed.
When I asked for the reason,
Everybody had given some reason or the other.
And, somebody had said it was due to the use of pesticides.
Well, why could you not convince them
That they were redundant so long as you were there?

And now after a long absence, here in this cold country
In Fall, you suddenly appeared and delighted me.
Oh! There is a flock around you.
Have you migrated here like me, perchance?
Hey, you are jeering at me in your wont way.
Thank heavens!
Have you recognized me, at last?

❖

RAVI VERELLY

No More Lives

Then:

There was no form.
There were no limits at all.
My term of life
Was the same as that of Milky Way.
I had full-fledged freedom
To touch the bourns of skies
And the depths of abysses same time.
My existence was
At the threshold of nine planets.

Now:

I am a prisoner serving life
Born in the cellar with nine doors.
The irony is
I am the guard, I am the judge
I have to serve the term, all alone.
Bound with shackles of affections,
Injecting into the veins
Selfishness boiling with desires
Is the punishment.
How long these decorated walls
Hoisting greed can stand?
In the battle of life
Between breath and death

A day shall come
When the jail shall have to close
If all that I can achieve
Is a lay on the roster of history
That the time machine rolls out,
I want no history
And I want no life.
God! Grant me endless freedom!

NANDA KISHORE

Revision 2

Some acquaintances are such!
Furnishing wings
You did not fancy in your wildest dreams
They bid you up suddenly
Pitting against gushing winds.

If you could somehow manage
To drop down safely, fine!
You can still breathe life
Even if your body is battered.

But if you continue your assay
For fun or in frolic
That's it!
Your ordeals and your odyssey
Commence instantly.

The sky continues to elude eternally,
No life runs smoothly on the land;
One has to fear the rain and wind,
And hie scared of an eagle or a snake.

One has to answer
The tree... if you build a nest,
The hill ... if you drink of a rill,
The field... if you glean few grains,
And the wind... if you molt.
Even if you plead innocence,

Saying you know nothing but flying,
Or pray flying is imperative for your living,
You have to apologize.
Speaking the language of the flowers,
Crooning in the voice of dove
Or talking in childy morpheme
Is not what you need to learn,
But to pretend as any human being does.

Crying wild and flying off to unknown shores
With a freedom of no consequence,
You have to answer
The tree, the field, the rill, and the wind.

And, answer you must!

❖

BHAVANI PHANI

Death Adrift

You are not my pal,
Nor did I even invite you here!

Didn't you hear mom saying
One shouldn't socialize uninvited?
Why do you tread upon my heels
And pester me?
There are many things for me to do.
I have to play with lovely butterflies;
And have to slip into sleep
Mooning about the moon;
Have to decorate my foreyard
With chalky designs
And dance with my pals
Around Gobbemmas for Pongal;
'Eyes of Palmyra Fruit' I have to savor;
Prepare and sundry condiments in mid-summer
Have to drench in the first spell of showers
For the inviting smell of the wet earth;
And put my ear to the resonating water
Streaming down the cement pipes;
Have to visit the temple of lord Shiva
And 'clap behind the deity';
Have to build sand houses
In the dunes of the dried up canal;
I have to don a silk petticoat;

Wear parandas in my hair;
Have to weave and wear in my braids
A garland of crossandra;
Have to receive prasadam
From granny in her holy attire;
And have to boil chick-peas
Distributed in propitiation on Sravan Tuesdays;
Have to twaddle in the veranda during power-cuts;
Or, sleep over the folding cots in the backyard;
Have to listen to stories about tom cat from granny
And pretend sleep if she frightens
That the cat's long tail takes us away, if we won't;
Have to make paste of henna leaves
And decorate stars in my palm
And threaten the thief of throwing him into the well
If the hand doesn't turn crimson;
Must recite Lalita Sahasram
At Poleramma temple
And gather the Parijata before all others did.

You Death! This is not your way...
I don't have time to argue with you.

❖

In the Footsteps

Did you notice?
No sooner had you come,
Than the moonlight assumed a strange glow!
The gravel road
Through the Casuarina plantation
Was eager to speak about
Yesterday's rain.
Shall we go out for a while?
Oh, no! Don't put such desperate face
You don't have to talk, OK?
Just give me company!
I love to watch, at least today
That cozying up pair of doves,
The evening lamp in the temple's niche,
And the blossoming rubia on the creeper,
With you beside me.
Before I essay my living
Afresh tomorrow,
Let me breathe for a while.
It's not far off.
Can we walk down?
I am sure
It would be clear to you
At least, while we return.
The closeness of breath
Doesn't connote intimacy.

❖

RADHIKA

My Village

May be
She felt my absence
The Fig Tree in the midst of the village
Had shed its leaves.

Maybe, it thought it was no more relevant
The stone bench had showed up cracks.

The temple-steps and the banks of the village tank
Seemed eagerly waiting for me.

There was no trace of the creaking
Of the rope swing laid to the guava tree

Perhaps they might have thought that I won't return,
Some close and dear
Had deserted the place.

Now, the village stands
A dilapidated testimony
To my history.

Oh! I shouldn't have gone there.
It would, at least, have remained lively in my memories.

PRASUNA RAVINDRAN

The Sky

The sky is
A great painter
Who draws upon herself
Umpteen self-portraits!

To the sky
Tired of baby-sitting
The Sun during the day, and
The Moon at night,
God shall permit a night off
Only on the new moon day.

Yet,
The sky shall not rest
But loses herself in gossip
Gathering all stars about her
Even as the night
Tries to lull her to sleep
Under its shroud.

◆

MANASA CHAMARTI

Solitude or Loneliness?

Even amidst a large gathering
This loneliness hurts me deep;
Even as I go in search of solitude
A vague idea treads on my trails.

The whole world is asleep... excepting me
Even the stream takes rest, suspending its giggles
And the recent agitation among the foliage is absent
And there is no trace of the warmth of the day... in the air.

The autumnal cloud throws the night-veil
Across the sky-line to dry;
Flaunting its brilliance under the moonbeam
It laughs in its sleeve, watching the gloomy-faced me.

Night melts before my very eyes
The stars disappear to different worlds
As the singular witnesses to the struggle within
Letters stream across the sheet like this.

❖

Translated from Telugu ● *NS Murty*   **245**

On Becoming Rain

Eons have passed
Landscapes have changed
But the nascent smell of the rain
Sinking into the earth has not changed.

How many feelings
Shall it spray
Springing back to life
Memories from the depths of heart!

For once
I long to turn into a cloudlet
And roll over in the dust...

VAMSIDHAR REDDY

Confessions of a Poet

So, tell me who you are?
Me?
I am an itinerant mammal with the
Processor medulla oblongata tucked in my brain.
I am a homo sapien wiser than monkey by about 12 points.
I am an animal hungrier than the wild
I am variously called a man
Dou you know? I am a man!

Hum! What do you do?
Nothing in particular.
I purge my awareness of being a man
While defecating in the open.
And if I was incensed
I search for any pleasing remains of humanity and annihilate.
But, I quench thirst with my own blood,
I had a near-fatal experience
When I changed the blood group
And if I am tired,
I stretch myself coolly nestling in somebody's thoughts.
That's all.

Why do you write?
When a silence
That decimates all expression sieges me;
Or when I feel there's nothing for me to speak;
Either to cover up my crimes;

Or if it fails, to conceal;
To blame or to torture myself;
To appear as complex as possible to myself.
On the oiled paper the chili-bajji was wrapped,
Or on the white tissue paper in the washroom
I scribble.
People say you write poetry on poverty draining scotch in AC rooms
And passionately orate about feminism treating your wife as slave at home
Well, when do you stop writing all this shit?
I don't.
Till one of us dies.
Till all the trees of the world are turned into paper
And stink with my effusions I will not;
Or, till the world praises me and pays tributes at my grave
I won't.

OK! OK! Let's conclude. For God's sake, tell me the truth?
Who are you?
After a long distressing silence
Pulling out some papers drenched in my sweat
I cry:
"I'm half human... and... and,
I am not a poet."

It's Hard to Vacate The Resident Silence

It was long
Since my reflection in the mirror smiled;
And god knows when
The dismal prospects crossed
The thresholds of imagination last!

Deep inside
Failure peeps through nervously

The word bandied from the lips
Ducks in some corner of the heart;
And the aborted thought splintered to smithereens
Aches and smarts within.

Sometimes, one has to explode the lips
With a claymore mines
To dig out the buried words.

In this compulsive living
I have to bear the burden of knowledge

Rolling up, I must hole myself up
Somewhere deep within.

Voice must break the walls of silence
Yet,
It is not that easy to vacate the resident silence.

Translated from Telugu ● NS Murty

Nothing Much to Say

1

Now there are only two tenses:
The times when I loved her,
And the times when I can't help loving her.

2

It never occurred to me how time would pass without her.
All these days, amidst enveloping despair,
I could understand I was better off because of her.
But strange, I could never understand her.

3

People say that I had changed remarkably since her friendship.
Very True. My lyric is for her; and my song is for her;
I kindle my heart and await her in darkness.
I assume a different bod every day and incinerate.
It's beyond anybody to imagine
The tragedy in possessing her and the blessing in losing.

4

Maybe, that there was life before seeing her is a fact.
But that was inanimate;
What if she had left me with a wound?
There's pleasure in reminiscing her
For turning me into a being.

◆

MAHESHKUMAR KATHI

My 'Gin'ny Devil

Emptying myself into the bottle
Putting the lid, I dropped myself in a time capsule.
I had experience; and knowledge enough.
But I remained in the bottle.

Did I waste myself?
Or molded myself into a model for the future?
Shall I reduce to an exhibit in a museum ultimately?
Or shall I dry up without trace? I don't know.

Devils come out if you open some lids.
But out of this bottle come the signatures of the past
And the memories of the present.
I am not sure if they be of any use to future.
But losing me to myself, I remained as time itself.

❖

MANASA CHAMARTI

The Liberated Nymph

Oh, Me! How tender you look!
The flower blushed as tenderly.

You must forever remain like this for my sake!
Pulchritude fluttered in delight.

Can you sing any lays?
Music turned its voice

Won't you bless me with a kiss?
Love embraced in consummating angst.

House should be kept spick and span.
Nature replicated itself in the foreyard.

Where do they stand before me?
Silence appropriated reticence.

I am totally lost! There's no way out!
Courage exhorted and reassured.

Don't show up your face to me again, I hate it!
Patience gulped down the insult.

Ay, you! Come here.
Passion startled and surrendered all it had.

It was an emotional aberration. What's wrong with that?
Friendship screamed under the burden of altar vows!

When did I say that you are everything for me?
Heart broke to smithereens.

The liberated Nymph let out a laconic laugh
 And left without cursing.

❖

MARUVAM USHA

Restless Traveller

When I look back now,
Behind me I see,
Miles-long amaranthine trail of life
I walked through to reach my temple of satiation.
It might be rough, rugged and patchy
Yet it was my becoming; and
People true, intimate and uninhibiting were the landmarks.
Tossed about the passage were
The hillocks of my successes;
Vales of despair and ladders of life's longings
That lifted me up from abysses;
Moments of merry broadcast by the treescape;
Plains of perennial flowers.
It was dotted with cactuses of agony,
Which even grief would refrain itself from.
It was an ineluctable marathon run,
No matter whether I was thirsty or tired.
Whenever I suspended the run to catch my breath,
Neither could I appropriate the sojourn,
Nor it turned out to be a breather.
There were scores of colleagues,
To the left, to the right, to the fore and behind,
Each going their own way,
Making no meritable streak on my touchstone.
Now, when I look ahead,
An inexplicable impulse seizes me to move forward.

Seas of disturbing nightmares and
Volcanoes of distresses have passed memory's reach.
Calling of meadows of fulfillment
And turfs of salvation is invitingly alluring.
Unto the last step of my journey,
I am a restless traveler.

❖

P VIDYASAGAR

Dushyanta Shall Not Return

You wait and wait endlessly for your Godot
The memories of yesterday's sweet insignia
Drown like paper boats in your streaming tears.
Easier than playing a lute without a string
Your Dushyanta plays with your body without wedding vows
And disappears like a picture on the silver screen.
When you look back
The cosmetic rouge peels off
And you remain abandoned alone
Like a tin of talcum cast off.
Like a python that has swallowed a buck,
He would run away leaving you a mistress
Devouring your youth and the attending bloom.
It's your inanity!
Pray as many gods as you may, but
Your Dushyanta shall never come to you.

You can put up with boycotts and hide your grief
Fine!
But how can you hide your billowing belly?
Whenever you stand before the mirror
Your reflection catechizes 'who fathers the foetus?'
The rolled-gold ring he pressed on your finger
Mocks at you losing its short-lived glitter.
As you try to scout for his whereabouts
You remember the counterfoil of cinema ticket

And the snapped sacred thread and feel betrayed.
Then you repent:
"Damn it!
How easily the powders and scents have conned!
And how the silk sari Dushyanta presented
Served as a blindfold for him to vanish."

Where is your Dushyanta, dear sis, where is he?
He must have already enticed your other sibling
Somewhere in a remote agency village!
In a fancy display of half-year's spousehood
He impregned you before retreating;
Grabbing these lands
As easily as he ensnared your body
And decamping with the produce
As "One of Seventy"* stood a mute witness.
Growing from foetus to a full limbed spirit,
The infant asks no sooner than it lands on earth:
Mother! When will father come back?
The question iterates through generations. Yet,
You shall await your Godot still.

*One of seventy (1/70): Is a land transfer act prohibiting outsiders
  purchasing tribal tracts in India.

❖

ABD WAHED

Market

This body is a garden of flowers
And the wounds are just small and big posies
The hum of the bees of political compassion around
Is but the malodor from the abscess... scented apurpose.
When life itself becomes so dreadful
Who cares for death but death itself?

What abode can a speck of dust have
Than go itinerant with the wind incessantly blowing it?
The firebrand-tongues inflame tongues of fire
Crying out... not to die of thirst.
Meditating Marabou sell faith for a price
Fish swim across to buy pints of water

Well, when your mien becomes businesslike
Even your passions and compassion get showcased.
Go! Sell tears to the bawler.

When once you start selling
Why secrecy,
Sell babies to the umbilical cord
Sell games of delusion on the slide of equivocacy.
If eyelids close for the glitter of the sword
Don't confuse it for the weariness of sleep
The lava under eyes continues to swell.
Should the pigeons of the Masjid negotiate peace?
The foundations of these Minars ramify the depths of earth
Now, there is no more fear of earthquakes.

◆

Wakes on The Horizon ● *A selection of poems*

PRASUNA RAVINDRAN

Once Again

Just as the skies repossess
The cloud they lost after it had rained out,
How nice would it be
If man could get back the dear ones he had lost!!

Just as the river
Re-flowing through the forgotten furrows
How great it would look if
The present could be diverted into the
Hollows of yesterday!!!

Though this is the cherished bank
Reached with relish,
Won't I give a taste of my childhood
Shaming every moment
Slipping with simmering discontent?

❖

BOLLOJU BABA

Death in a Hospital

A soul gets liberated from body shackles with a swan song.

"Woe betided me, Mother!
How could you leave us,
Having lived your whole life for us?"
A son was grieving effusively with matchless histrionics,
Who till yesterday treated her like a housemaid.

On the countenances of other patients
Fear spread like an acrid spray
The smell of cold death pervaded the ward
As resignation, philosophy and karma took over.
Closing his eyes, an old man was visualizing
A world-without-him on an imaginary screen.

The eyeballs of a paralytic,
Lying helpless like an ox under shoeing,
Rolled out tears... with jealousy.
"Ay! Don't go that way!"
A woman in childbed bids her elder boy
Whom she wants to see as a doctor.

The heart of a relative moans with yearning
Cursing the patient for standing
In his way of reaching for the coveted grapes.
It seems the bargain was not settled. For,
The purse of the kin of the deceased is still heavy
And the pocket of the ward-boy is still empty.

Perplexed about who to contact and how
The cadaver-carrying rickshaw-puller smelling death,
Is dithering at the window
Like an uneasy kitten in front of a latched kitchen.

"This body is a leather bellow with nine cavities..."
The coughing mendicant cants a philosophical strain
And gulps syrup about a dram... after the bout.

One customer is lost
To the bat-infested lodge beside the hospital,
To the medical shop across the road,

To the round-the-clock hotel abetting the wall,
And to the empty-bottle selling old hag
Shriveled like a salted fish.

A swan perched on a remote tree
Takes off to the skies with a snigger.

RAVI VERELLY

_____

Severally

In the absence of whiffs of breeze
That punctuate the air with fragrances,
Two flowers blooming to the same sprig
Shall experience impassable reaches
Like the two detached gold discs hanging severally
To the thrice knotted sacred thread, sagging
Under the weight of diverging lateral thoughts.

With the light and darkness
Lying like Siamese twins
Under the sheet of firmament,
We remain two perfectly sundered halves
When the yarns of necessities
Fail to conjugate us double hard

Though we are pieces of the same cloth
We retain our identity intact
In the quilt of rags that time mends.

Like the Longitudes and Latitudes
Which notionally join a world
Divided at its very natal hour,
Come! Let us revolve round and round
Along with the earth, severally.

◆

The Two of Us Know

When you wash the dirt,
Naturally, a little spills over to stain you.
People who say 'phew' and walk away
May call you dirty.

When you kindle a fire
Few sparks flare up
To singe you.
People who do not walk their talk
May blame you are warming by the fire

When you stand up for the truth
You can't escape
The looks of suspicion
Inured as they are to lies
People, for sure, take you for an accomplice.

You know that
You swim against the current
Stand challenging the whirlwinds
And unflinchingly confront selfishness;

You know
That it is more important to fight than to win.

And so do I know
It is unfair to give up fight than to surrender.

Translated from Telugu ❧ *NS Murty*   **263**

This is not a highway for people to accompany
But a razor's edge;
This is not mutual admiration to lend voice
But a thunderous cry in contempt.

This is not the path we chose abruptly now.
Why should we then worry, friend?
We know that every step we put
Is a step forward;
Perhaps only we two know.

We are prepared for this lonesome ruffled journey
But when we reach the shore
We launch the anchor, right on his heart!

◆

A Man Without Face

He does possess an anatomical heart,
But it shall never throb

Amidst embarrassing necessities
He shall always be weaving
A cobweb of relationships.
Occasionally,
We can hear him
And, also, see his actions.
The only thing that we cannot see
Is his face.

In fact,
He was long dead
For goodness
And for humanity.
He is always in the look out
For excuses to hate
Just as the village, for loving him.

Even when every minute that has passed
Every word he has uttered
Accost him;
Every path he crossed
And every step he put
Follow him from a winking distance

Translated from Telugu ● *NS Murty*

Walking over concrete
He turns as hard-hearted as concrete;
And petrifies, after taking waters of civilization.
The man who took leave of the village once,
Leaves it once for all.

◆

MOHAN RUSHI

War and Peace

They bequeath us some epochal texts
Some new jargon, new expertise
Some twilight hymns
Some aural parting days
And some exotic worlds.

Thanks.
For expanding and sharpening our vision;
Being another milestone in the journey of life
And, for resurrecting us once more.
Here begins our uninhibited journey...
Until another one seizes us with their philosophy
Or
Till we leave ourselves behind
Shaking off this mundane bod

KATTA SRINIVAS

Timeless Journey

World won't end if all material things cease,
But when thinking ceases,
No matter how much matter is left,
The world ends!

Time shall not stop
Just because you throw away all clocks.
The day when motion stops
It ends abruptly on its own!!

Just for the absence of greetings
Friendships won't taper.
They come to nought
When there are no memories left!!!

◆

K LINGA REDDY

Mother Earth

Clearing woods, bush and bramble
A field is made of fallow.
This parched thirsty glebe
Watches the skies above agape.
Greenhorns stagger
To drive the harnessed plough;
Seed broadcast like chalky patterns in the foreyard.
But when time rages and skies go barren
Shoots wither in the seed and the land cracks dry.
When hungry kids are put to sleep
Grief spills over to the brim of eyelids.
The earthen levee caves in;
Silt settles in the farm well;
The rope of the bucket snaps
And the pulley idles forever.
Corns grow on feet;
Blisters rise in hands;
The cart of life
Sinks in the mire of *Anantavagu*.

Well desilted
Its inner lining bulwarked
Silver anklets melt away;
Electric pole erected
Electric motor fixed
Cowshed becomes desolate;
The dextral ox of the yoke is foot-injured;

The nigh ox is sold to slaughter-house.
The pen is looted; but all bovine
Appear in *Gajwel* animal fair.
Tiled roof blows off;
Decrepit house leaks;
Kitchen room caves in
So does the head of the household.
No God comes to the rescue.
No propitiation brings in blessings.
Be it the milk poured in snake holes
Victuals given to *Katta Maisamma* under the Neem tree;
The lamb sacrificed to village Goddess;
Or, the family god of Siddulagutta
Nobody comes to dry your tears.

The village tank breaches.
The rill runs dry.
Fissures show up in the *Summer-plot*
The motor burns out.
Current bill soars.
Agriculture takes crop holiday.
The hard money loan not made good;
Lender reaps insults by
Public-auctioning utensils, and
Running away appropriating the main doors...
Poor children!
They live out the hard times
Surviving trading blood for life.
Even when the "Vinegar Pot" was empty
I avowed not to sell my land.
But, when fate turns against you
State turns out to be a cancerous cell
Conspicuously on the "land of wells"
Manifests the tumor of real-estate.

◆

What Does He Do Alone?

Suffering the turmoils within
What does he do alone?
Sitting on the sandy shore
He would pen poems on the spurgy tides;
Going lyrical at the undulating waves and the swaying froth
He would hum a tune striking rhythm with their balletic steps.
When the tide overwhelms him
He would be perturbed like a fry
And if life also recedes from him with the tide.
He hides cozily in sands like any other cowrie.
He would never reveal to anybody
That the Sea was in love with him;
Nobody would ever make out
That he had longed for the turmoil.
All that would ever be known about him is...
That he is no more.

❖

TUMMALA DEVA RAO

Festival of Rain

On the bare barren lands.
On the expanse of green rice corns,
Over the roofs of the thatched hovels,
And upon temples and glazing marble mansions
Comes down heavily the rain
In streams, currents and torrents.

Rain is a paradigm of equality principle,
A shuttle of water wool
Stitching the earth and heaven together,
A midwife attending soil's labour,
A divine leaf-sap restoring vigor
To the greying moribund landscape.

Rain
Is an old primogenitor to both farmer and the farm;
Rain
A delectable spectacle of droplets landing on land
As watery lamps, as its heart bursts out.
Rain
A close pal of children
Who voyage their childhood on paper boats
An ambassador to couples
Trading sweet heart-throbs
Huddling under an umbrella;

Rain ...rain ...rain
Over dust and dirt

272

Threading and flooding rain
Inhaling the scents of wettish earth.
A Mother cow welcoming the calf of capering wind
Caressing its back licking with tongues of showers.
A young bride drawing chalky designs
Over the surface of the lake with silvery dust.
A mischievous hammer battering the mountains.

Rain
Streaming down...and spinning down
Like a poem... a folklore... a garden of stars
Like a rainbow!
Come on children
Out into the open leaving your schools and shrines!
Let us frolic in the carnival of rain!
Come on little sparrows
Come out of your nests!
Let's slake our dried up hearts
With droplets skiing down the cornices.
Let's put our ears to the soft thrum
Of rain drops beating on the blades of grass!
Men and women! Come out!
Liberate yourselves from your concrete cells
Let's witness the musical extravaganza played on the grasslands
And present our natural selves afresh
Stemming the corruption of our affections.

❖

MAHESHKUMAR KATHI

Wailing Half-naked

Exact to the Archimedes' Principle
My heart burdened with your memories
Has spilled an equal volume of tears through eyes...
Your death
Has made me more inert
Than working up an equal and opposite reaction.
Did Newton go wrong for a change?
Or, your melting into the void
Has made an exception to his principle?

The rational mind
Has searched for the reason behind heart's mien;
Looking for solace,
It tried to measure the interminable vacuum.
The flames on your pyre flared high...
And to douse the heat,
Films of cloud gathered round my eyes.
I sat there half-naked with streaming tears.
Then I realized:
How badly needs a wailing man his shirt.

◆

PRASUNA RAVINDRAN

My Lone Moments

Singing lullabies to the Day
Tired of dragging the heavy moments,
And putting it to sleep
A private spring wakes up for me, and me alone.
Though the sleep knocks at the threshold
Donning the dream-knit sari,
When I recall that it was ages since I last caressed the word,
I throw open the door first.

The Moon spreading the carpet of moonlight and
The wind spraying the perfumes, walk in my wakes.

Listening to the jingle of my steps,
The garden quietly goes all abloom.

Don't know why,
The crumbs of cloudlets dropped down in anger
And stampeded all along the way
Seem to hum some teasing unknown strain.

I am tempted to make a bonfire here
Searching words for some past torpid emotion.
What a rare moment is this confluence of darkness and silence!
If only I had known the language of the cricket,
Perhaps, I could find a flood of vocab I cannot put down.

Like a pellicle of cloud
Excited over its first hug from Moon, gleaming wherever it goes,

Translated from Telugu ● NS Murty   **275**

Like a breeze...
Melting lay sweeping through the woods taking a hue from it,

The memory of that lone sweet word you said
Splitting into several echoes
Eased through my warm breath subjecting me to its charm,
Sweeps over me caressing the locks on my forehead;

All through the day,
I eagerly await these moments of peerless loneliness
When they lift me up and cuddle in their embrace.
Gleaning few exotic petals,
I walk back to my window in great contentment.

◆

PULIPATI GURUSWAMY

Anand

*'D*addy! Don't you sing me a song?'
Hailed Anand from the entrance
Even before he walked into the room.
I was just wondering at his unusual request.
He must have guessed it from my silence.
He said, *'all my classmates are singing for an event.*
It's is only me who knew no songs.
Will you teach me one, daddy?'
'I am sorry, Anand, neither do I.
I can read you a poem if you like.'
'Then sing me a poem.'
"A son unkind to his parents
Counts for little whether he is dead or alive
Won't termites in an ant hill exist and go extinct?"
I did not complete.
"Thuuuuu..." he said bitterly putting up a sour face.
"What song is this daddy?" He did not hide his contempt.
"What can I do? I know only this."
I answered rather apologetically.
"Pch..." he uttered holding his head
In the crescent of his thumb and index finger.
After a while,
"At least, do you know how to dance?"
 "No," I said.
(One can guess the consequences if I had said yes.)
Shaking his head rather uneasily, he asked rather coolly,

"Then what do you know daddy?"
There was a hint of despair and hopelessness in the voice.
My worst fears came true. I was in pits.
He asked finally, *"Do you know swimming?"*
"God!' ... My heart creaked. Soul rattled within.
My daughter began laughing at the other end of the room.
He closely watched the changing colours in my face.
"Go! Get lost in your poetry."
And left.

❖

The Compassionate Resolute

The preserve of eyelids
Could neither constrain the dreams,
Nor contain the streaming tears.

Any number of moments
Have been swept away by that ceaseless flow.

Now, the heart is like the clear sky
With its cloud cover unveiled.

Just as meaning nestles into graphemes,
Words dissolve in silence at this moment.

❖

Sometimes

Sometimes...

Losing a battle inspires you more than winning it;
A censure excites you more than an undue praise;
The darkness feels more soothing than the sunshine.

Sometimes...

You feel like opening your heart out to utter strangers;
It looks a smile answers enough than a reply;
An urge overwhelms to believe things blindly.

Sometimes...

It feels amnesia is a fitting end to a haunting past;
Tears deem true partners in despair;
Heart yearns for loneliness than any company.

Sometimes...

You love listening to pleasing lies than tarty truth;
You long to look for comfort in agony itself;
Silence seems supreme to saying something...

◆

SRINIVAS VASUDEV

You Scurry off...
Leaving Me to My Music

Even as I plead that
The word rots on the edge of the nib
Or, an idea hiccups in the gullet,
You care a toss and scurry off
Condemning me searching for you
In the Tiananmen Square, or
In the Bougainvilleas!
I have expected to find you
In the quietude of tomb dug by silence within, or
In the chirping of the cricket for its mate...
I search for you in
The Hibiscus asleep...
The sigh divorced from me... and, in the
Call of the birds tucking freedom under their plumes...
I search unabashedly
Thinking that you might have been caught
In the improbable shadows
And behind unreasonable soft wear
O You, the streak thought disengaged from me!
O You, that follow me like a shadow!
I look for your wakes
In the crown of the firefly that visits
At an unknown hour of the night...
And in the smiles of the night queen

Peeping through the dark nightly windows
For a freezing idea?
Or for the bloodless coup of a Cross
To come to the rescue of hunger and discrimination?
Thus lasts my yearning
Among the medley of words
For strains of my own cerebrations...

◆

Like a Dream of the Night

All of a sudden
I hit upon some page
Where I find myself there.

From the book inverted
Silence dribbles memories.
As the tips of the fingers sift the mind through
What can I write about this moment?

Some moments can never be put down! That's all!

Yet, there's something to write about...
Apart from truth, terra and day
Or fancy, firmament and night
Something like the chaotic world
That slips heavily through the eyelids
At the night after the second watch...
Something ephemeral like a Higgs Boson
As trillions of particles collide all at once
Something akin to life's journey
Which we long to revisit on occasion
But it never occasions and we march ahead
There's something for sure
May not be the destination, though.
There must be some aura
More awesome than the tune we could catch

Or the haunting expression we wanted to write.
Like a drop of rain trickling from nowhere,
Like the dream of the night we forget first in the morning
It remains elusive still
Is it a song? Or a sound?

KONDAMUDI SAIKIRAN KUMAR

Epiphany

Sky wraps itself
In a mantle of Darkness

Emotion besieges
All imagination

The lone tree
Contends with wind

The mind
Fights in quietude

What a glorious silence!

There is neither fear
Nor pain
No venting of anger
Over helpless moments
Not to speak of any
Unseasoned bliss

The most surprising, however is...
My waking within.

Translated from Telugu ◈ NS Murty

A Handshake

Here is my diary
With every page full...
Helloing me
Shaking hands in cool reticent words;
Like tears greeting streaming silently
I empty memories
And jettison the
Vacuous moments.

Let not dreams fluster anymore...
An exotic effulgence shall spread over the canopy
And the cloud encrusting moonshine shall disperse.
In a life as expansive as the heavens
A pattering drizzle
Springs heart back to life.

Now the clock ticks
Moments unburdened
And the body
Rests without nightmares.

Unobtruded by companionship
Cions of warbling imagination shoot up
I create now,
Time immeasurable... for my own sake.

◆

With the Yoke You Left Half-way

That the necessities were welling up each year
Like water in a spring,
And the loans were growing wild with interest
Like reed unattended,
You took to liquor once
To drown the worry;
But today you took this "peasanti-cide"
And dropped down dead like a pest.
Ever since you merged into the elements
Leaving me to get drenched in the storm;
Left me as the lone prop
For the parents who begot you
And for the children we begot
Ignoring that I was behind you for everything
From the day our lives were tied together,
I have been spiriting myself each day
To buck up and hang on…
The hands that never turned up for help
When you were alive,
Have flocked around me;
And are hovering still,
With looks of hunger like hawks and raven
Around weak and emaciated;
The sufferings you thought
Would cease with your decease
Have only thrown us from the pan into the fire.

Translated from Telugu ● *NS Murty*   **287**

Like the chatter of cicadas at midnight,
Harassment of creditors
Heart-rending hunger cries of children
And the 'un-cloakable' youthful graces
Refrain unceasingly;
Fear, want and emptiness
Linger in the dried up eyes
Like the traces of water in a farm well.

To unveil the dawn of sensibility in our people
I must fence the looks converging on me,
Put fire into my looks
And stop them in their tracks;
Lugging the yoke you left half-way
I must culture the field of life
To survive
And I continue to survive...
Until I reach the other bank
Swimming with the lone hand
I live
And continue to live.

♦

KODURI VIJAYAKUMAR

In the Dark Room

That night...
When failures banished sleep
To the eves of eyelashes;
When this wounded body sang blues
All night with darting pain;
Death, escorted by rain,
Entered the dark room and said:
"Friend! Look here!
Your grief is a ceaseless torrent!
Life is but a bout of grief... nothing more;
Come! Hug me!
Let me anoint your wounds in my embrace!"

Some harsh words
Emanated through the wounds:
"This soil of my motherland
Was steeped in the blood of my heroes
Where even ploughs were turned
Into weapons on occasion;
This is my abode, I am a man that adore people that fight;
Fie! I can't be timid now as to embrace Death.
I can't insult the sacrifices of my martyrs."

There was a rumbling of thunder somewhere.
The doors were thrown open with a clatter.
There was neither rain... nor death.
The room was filled with sudden brilliance.

❖

Where Else is my Carkless Repose?

Woods are my birth place
There are comrades every way
Silken carpets of green pastures
Delicate dangling of baby branches
Ornate flowery ornaments
Fluting whispering winds
Concerts of wings on flight
Choreography of cascading steps...

I am a contented soul in my dominion.

❖

BALA SUDHAKARMOULI

Weaving the Dreams

As darkness
Slowly settles over there
Like a thin veil of raiment
They would sit weaving
Their dreams into
Exquisitely beautiful arcades
With equally splendid exchange of words.
Time
When people isolate themselves into
Diverse polarized worlds
Is indeed a delectable spectacle
To see them
Absorbed
And lost to themselves.
This night
The duo of mother and daughter
Look like two moons have
Risen on the horizon of their shack.

Where were they
Days before?
Yesterday?
They knew not.
Today
They are on the bourns of the village.
They are eternally itinerant.

*Translated from Telugu * NS Murty*   **291**

World is their abode
And the sky
Is their roof.

In the distant past
When some village expelled them
They reached this place like flotsam;
Learnt weaving the nest with bamboo
And somehow swim through the life.

What do they talk
The mother and her twelve-year old girl
In the evenings every day, anyway?

Is it
By the way,
About her studies?
Or
About her younger sibling
Living far off
In a hostel?
Or
About the vacant plot
Still available
Where they can
Erect a shanty?

Close by
Propping up the trellis
Sagged on one side, and
Weaving their dreams from the other end
Is the father
Of that lettered moon-doll.

RAVI VERELLY

Gravity

That silently dissolving drop of rain
Planting a wet kiss on earth's forehead
Gushes out like a fountain high someday

Peeping through mother twigs
And catching at the melting seasons
The rustling leaf speaks only after fall.

The cynosure of all eyes, the flower
Meditating on one leg over the stalk
Surrenders to the ripples of wind
To pay its respects to mother earth.

Cultivating the expansive field of firmament
And planting the seeds of stars, the Moon
Stretches her hands below to caress the crests of waves
To sprinkle a few drops of water

For me,
Shuttling between thought and theme
With dream-filled eyes,
It's a pleasure to hug you
Like the leaf
The flower
The drop
And the moonshine over the wave.

❖

Translated from Telugu ● *NS Murty*   **293**

PRASUNA RAVINDRAN

Memories

At least
When the sepia photos on the wall mock at us
We should suck into the past like whirlwind
Rather than coolly bypassing it like a river.

Like a streak of light
That squarely questions each oversleeping bud,
Memories scout for and catch at
The inmost roots of our existence
Which we ourselves are unaware
To present us eternal springs.

MERCY MARGARET

What is the Gender of the Seed?

It is a vast expansive ocean of verdure
How many leaves have been collected to create this!
How many trees have been felled!!
And how many saplings needed to be planted!!!
The waves that crash on its shores
Are but the flotsam of dry leaves
Which have lost their vigor,
And the ocean shall not covet them anymore;
She assigns to the winds the duty
To dribble up the mess every time.
That Ocean
Seems so pacific always to watch
Giving an illusion of cool and green;
But, within would be raging
Infernal Volcanoes
Earthquakes,
Animal and human sacrifices ...endlessly.
Then all of a sudden, one day,
A half-felled tree
Sprouts a leaflet
All barren and effete stumped up logs
Start the grapevine in whispers:
For all that, and all that
What is the gender of the seed
That impregnated the tree?
Is it female or male?

Yesterday's Dream

"How come you smell so sweet?"

Your compliment at nightfall
While your hand girdles my waist;
Lips blossom
Unable to conceal the excitement.

A similar night... even more fragrant

Monumental indifference without a turn of head
Works up a smooth silent wound.
Tears spill over
From an already heavy heart.

Bliss to the limits of the sky once
A grief of oceanic proportions now
On both occasions... you are the comrade
Do the embarrassed moments
Slipping silently away have any idea
Which of them is more unbearable?

MANASA CHAMARTI

The Monsoon Nights

The monsoon nights let not sleep a wink.

With the drops of rain suddenly pecking at the ground...
The earth tingling anew all over bathed in flowers...
And the sweet trilling of a dove in its nest with its mate
Let not sleep a wink the monsoon nights.

The thorn of chill prickles ever so gently
And the mischievous drizzle gets people wet slowly...
The wings remain in flight through the night
Till the twinkling glass-house gets blurred and hazy.

This rhythm in the back ground as lights retire
Stirs up memories of some ancient melody
Whirling steadily within like the scents of the soil
Bidding goodbye to the month-long love-sickness

The delicate entwines around the tender waist
Locks on the forehead caressing the un-veiled bosom
Oh! What dreamy scripts the tips of nails encrypt, but
The blue eyes go all aglow... and the lightning to cloud nine.

Monsoon nights let not sleep a wink.

Ethereal Vision of the Melody

Heralding the day to
The statues and the ruins,
The sea and the city
Dawns pleasantly quivering
He was heard on flute

Following the wakes of melodies
In the lake of serene air
I searched for and found him...
Did I really find him?
No! He deigned to appear.

When the tunes had ceased
And he folded up the bag
I felt
If he had folded up the city of
Mahabalipuram also along.
Leaving the throbbing mornings to music
Had he embraced nights for his observation?
I did not ask. For, I know,
Silence is just an extension of meditation.

It was late into the night;
I offered to accompany him to his house.
He smiled silently... perhaps, suggesting
"Aren't you aware that darkness is my Siamese twin?"
On the eve of bidding adieu

I asked him among other things:
Why didn't you enter the temple?

How many times ever I ask him the question
With an ecstatic pleasure
Beyond the realm of senses he would whisper:
"It's a secret, sir!"
"Enakku imgaye darsana maagum"
("I see the lord from here.")
In a gesture of obeisance he groped
For his seven eyes... on the flute.

The Sublimity of Life

The first cloud that skims along
The last whiff of summer breeze
Leaves an impression of verdurous kiss
On earth's parching lips.

The cold wind that comes riding
Over the last drop of rain
Passes off... blessing each body
With an encounter of warmth

The summer born
In the ultimate moments of winter
Recedes throwing a fistful of jasmines on adults
And a chestful of memories to children

Novelty of life and the tapering of death
Shall always fine tune
The music of life
Love always
Enlivens the passages of life
With its fragrances

What a sublime life it is
When we humbly subject to time or love
And surrender our being and our existence!!!

Unrelenting Drizzle

As the wind blows off the roof,
I run after the wheeling palm leaves...
The delight at the gust of rain-borne wind
Evaporates in no time.

As the waters enter the house,
I try bailing out with utensils.
The indulgence of rain drops
Really takes me to my wit's end.

One should only witness skies emptying!
Tut!
No matter whether you stand or sleep,
You cannot avoid getting wet.

My pa goes out to break the farm bunds.
Yes! Otherwise, at the time of weeding
It will be hell of a job to uproot the grass.

My ma
Tries to keep the hearth dry and warm;
For, even to stand idle
One needs few gulps of gruel.

Those wet swallows and the young sibling
Chirp silently grinning in glee...
While we struggle to plug the leaks on one side,
The nuisance of having to put up with their noise on the other.

In the crevice of the hand-mill
A water-snake sneaks and peeps through.
Who cares whether it is spring
Or, some other damn season.

Where under the rafters
These rats hid all along, no one knows.
Snakes swim across in rounds... about the house.

Whatever the government records show
About the working of its schools,
They close once the stream Morancha overwhelms.

Nothing happens to cattle and buffalo
It's only us humans
That shiver with cold.

Whether it takes a year or lifetime
Don't care
But I must somehow arrange
For a tiled-roof.

Everything including the rice-bag
Has gone wet.
How to tear paper and make boats of it?

For the reverberations of every thunder
Walls slowly give way coming off in flakes and clods...
Where is the time to prop, patching them up with clay?

◆

SWARAJYAM RAMAKRISHNA

A Friend Indeed

It flickers last on the long drawn-out list of requirements.
But, it has its settled place in my pocket
Like the stretched string on a Veena.
Drying my eyes and concealing my sighs within its layers,
It takes into its sure sweet hands
The momentous events of my life.
Standing by me in the thick and thin of the day
And never settling comely where it was put
It embraces me dearly
With love and concern
Only to get tarnished in return
With the shades of my sad and solemn moments.
Be it the droning swarm of hovering mirages,
Or the aroma of my fruitless love,
Or the fears and passions erupting out of sudden happenings
Why
It absorbs every single secret of my life into its fold
And waits on me, ever so eagerly
Extending a guileless friendly hand.
When sun is at his singeing best over the crown
It sponges over the perennial springs of sweat
Planting a deep endearing kiss and restores sanity.
At great gatherings, parties and while on travel
It always books me a seat at no cost
And becomes a handy wave of flag at see offs.
No matter whether I caress it gently spraying scents

Or, wriggle and crumple and cast it off,
It waits a lifetime for my care and attention.
Unmindful of who calls on, it serves as selflessly
And stands out a symbol of love and fraternity.
It's why I commend:
Present a hanky whomsoever you love.

◆

ANIL DANI

Tête-à-Tête With Silence

Sh! No Noise!
I am in conversation with
My silence.
Submitting to the dictates of my conscience
I am reconning and counting
My mistakes in my silence
And trying to address them.

It's time
To take tougher decisions...
I am reinventing myself
Where I lost my way.

Well,
Be that it is God, friends or the world,
Circumstances or necessity
That had enticed and prompted me to my mistakes,
But ultimately
It was me who did
And I need, and correct myself.

Collecting one after another
The evils I strew so liberally across the cosmos
I am reaching out to the viable opportunity
To atone
Searching for myself
In my taciturnity.

❖

Translated from Telugu ● *NS Murty*

PRASUNA RAVINDRAN

Flapping of the Wings

As I tune up my heart
With the silence of the night

A Swan flapping its wings
Is heard over the pond.

Childhood
Revisits the lips...

Oh, this moment,
How sweet it breathes!

◆

You, Sculptor of my Life!

You, sculptor of my life!
You assigned to each organ of my body
A specific movement after recasting each...;
Whether you did it by an inadvertent error
Or, by intention as they were looking bad,
You have reoriented my eyes.
Now,
They should only watch the world you show
And that world is nothing but you.
O sculptor of my life!
Is it sufficient if I move
As your joystick-eyes guide,
Like a game toy made by you?
What about my spirit?
Do you wonder
How the statue can claim a soul?
Instead of acting as per your bidding?!
You sculptor of my life!
You blessed me these eyes...
You endowed me with vision... but,
You say, the world is only what you show;
And I shouldn't mind about my mind.
Isn't it you who shaped my lips?
Then why there should be speech,
When there is a head that can nod?
Strange indeed!

When I watched the world
Through my mother's lap,
I was like any other person.
There was freedom in my look,
There was freedom in my speech,
So was my laughter and my walk.
A platonic love,
As pure and voluntary as mother's,
Was available in abundance.
I was having that 'self' even when
They sent me after you in good faith.
When I was transformed,
Or,
When you metamorphosed me,
I know not!
You became the mentor
And I, the dancing doll
To dance to your dictates.
What a life!
There are eyes... but no vision,
There are ears... but cannot hear
There is voice... but cannot speak
There is a Soul... is as good as not,
Tut!
Can you still call this life???

MOHANRUSHI

Zero Degree

He never entertained any great hopes, but,
He searched for traces of originality in people.
In the way they speak, they do, they walk
Or the way they respond with compassion to a beggar
Encountered suddenly on their way

In their love, anger, passion or hatred,
Or the way they converse with a former valentine
Met at the old bus stand after a very long time.

"Huh! No use... aping has pervaded the cosmos
Between earth and heaven like ether..." he murmured.
How pleasant, once, he felt the footsteps of people approaching,
Like the bell of a sugar-candy-trolley to the ears a child; and
How he had watched them keenly, followed them
Sometimes catching them unawares and finally rued it was all in vain.

"Strangely, it is the veils that unveil the deficiencies
And the make-up that betrays the ugliness...
The more you pretend to show you have what you have not,
The more palpable will be the have not that you have not..."
He rather uttered the aside aloud.

He found nobody around, but he was sure he had heard
Someone strongly censuring: "Shut up! You silly fellow!"

❧

PRASUNA RAVINDRAN

At the Threshold of Heart

All this while...

As I struggled to wriggle out of
The bear-hug of the Computer
Where I was inaudible to myself

How long this torrential rain
Had been knocking at the door!
I don't know.
But, it rushed on to me
Planting an unexpected kiss
On my cheeks...

From hence
My heart shall be busy
Celebrating.

I Still Feel His Hand on my Shoulder

I still feel his hand on my shoulder

I still feel we were walking together
On that road... less travelled
He used to climb over the deer-like hillocks
With his piercing cheetah-like looks...

I still feel his hand over my shoulder.
When he laughed sweetly
Lending his hand
I felt the moon were in my reach

I still feel his hand over my shoulder
When he talked,
The love and devotion of a farmer
For his cultivation reflected and touched a chord in me

I still feel his hand over my shoulder
As he subtly rendered
The elegiac lays making tiresomeness
And the distance imperceptible...

I still feel his hand over my shoulder
He always appeared to me
Like a coveted lover or a friend
And been a great solace.

I still feel his hand over my shoulder.

Oh my dear enemy!
That profile of his
With his fist raised as the bullet pierced his heart
Still steals my sleep.

I still feel his hand over my shoulder.

◆

I Teach

Yes, I teach a lesson.
Oh! It is not new.
I have been teaching for ten years.
True! Let me admit it.
There was audacity and rebellion in that.

The student aspires to become an engineer
Or a doctor or some such thing,
But shouldn't he become a human being first?
How else than rebellious, can I teach him?
What else shall I teach him, other than life?
Should I not teach him about the crossroads,
And explain which way leads him where?
Isn't after he knows who laid the road for what end
That he can tread the way of his intend?
Shouldn't he, after all, be made aware that there were
Lives wagered for him and me?
Sacrifices that never expected in return a comforting tear?
That there were songs that woods reverberate with
And banished ballads upholding uncomfortable truths?
That there are battles that never cease with the deceased?

Yes, I admit, there was audacity and rebellion in my lesson,
But I am doing what I am supposed to do
And teach what I am supposed to teach.
Am I not supposed to stir up their conscience
Why songs sink in the gullet,

Dreams dry up at the threshold of eyes,
And campfires die out at midnight?
Shouldn't they think and think over again?

Unless one knows the drama going on the stage
How can one gauge the import of the roll he has to play?
There might be an interlude... a dragging silence
Between the refrain and the rhyme
Between two successive verses...
Shouldn't he learn to be patient enough to wait?

May be, at some unexpected turn
He may come face to face
With treachery and get hurt;
Shouldn't I infuse some un-impairing faith in him?
A companioning footstep may cease or retrace
Should I not inspire him not to lose heart?
I am just doing what I am supposed to do
And teaching what I am expected to.
Yes, the lesson is somewhat rebellious. So what?

◆

PRAVEENA KOLLI

Absurd Painting

It's a medley of colours smeared
Of ideas, ensconced in the inmost layers of the mind,
Hanging on to the tip of the brush for long and
Dropped and splattered in a dream.
Who knows
If the infinities at the centers of circles
And emotional upsurges in the haphazard strokes
Betoken
Lust or infatuation
Love or hatred
Spirit or lifelessness...?
Interpretations... unintelligible
Ambiguities... endless.
The figure drawn
In the stillness of the silent shadow,
Was hanging for long by the tip of the nib
When deep within heart there was an upheaval of unrest,
And thoughts billowed like a restless sea
And were caught in a clueless tangle...
Who could say
If it is grace or grief that face betokens
When it looks different every time you look at it?
Therein that picture
All strokes stretch without end or epoch
Like my thoughts;
Lines are in the lookout for a direction

Translated from Telugu ● *NS Murty*   **315**

Like my dreams;
And all images dissolve into nothingness
Like death.
The absurd painting hanging on to the wall in my room
Is just like me... my facsimile.

◆

VAMSIDHAR REDDY

Message Through Clouds

Oh! It looks it might rain any time.
When two oppositely-charged clouds interact
What reaches us first, thunder or lightning?
Velocity of sound is lesser than light, they say.
Where is my *bava?*
Thanks to Einstein...
Clouds are veritable thieves, no doubt.
Stealing water from the sea, and amassing,
Get heavy, lazy and lame
And vomit it on us...
Tat! Why doesn't a good simile strike me ever?
There it is, the first drop of rain
Tumbling down with terminal velocity
Thinking of breaking some head.
Why does a rain drop take the shape of a sphere?
Maybe, to reduce its surface tension,
Otherwise, won't it break down to smithereens?
Perhaps, this is what they meant
When they said life is but a bubble.
Charge! Prepare for the battle!
Reminding the music of war scenes in a movie;
Filling nostrils with the scent of first drops on earth
Comes rain pouring down heavily.
How many houses might have caved in?
And how many people might have died, who knows?
The Mahabharata story of rock pigeon *Jarita*
And her son *Jaritari* flashed in my memory for once

Translated from Telugu ● NS Murty

317

And touched a chord somewhere.
News item flashes in the dailies next day:
"Rain sweeps away nine lives...
Heavy rains lead to cholera in agency...
Farmers left high and dry."
Ranganayakamma should be informed
That rain is a bourgeois,
For, all ills somehow, converge only to BPL.
As for me
I fondled the drizzle with my fingers
Through the balcony grills,
Blissfully taking tea with *Pakodi*
And humming a childhood rhyme; or,
Was leaving paper boats in the streams; or,
Entertaining dirty ideas about taking advantage of rain
Chewing the sweetcorn to the limits in the eat-street
With the girl friend; or,
Draining down the 90 ml,
Dipped in the KFC or sand-witched by the McD burger
Was pretending my share of grief
For the devastation caused by the rain.
You lord of the clouds! Just one request!
Please give your priority to villages, not to towns.
Otherwise, we don't get anything to eat.
"You fool!" he replied
"Your towering buildings,
And the signal towers in towns,
The dust and pollution...
Stop, trap and harvest my water
What is there in a village... after all?
Neither a tree nor house worth mentioning.
Take note, fellow!
Your globalization has boomeranged on you!"
It was like a modern version of *"Meghasamdesam"*
Unveiling a universal truth.

◆

While Returning

I did not realize it
When infatuation for words seized me
Amidst incense clouds of experience
Nor did it strike me
When the whirling stream of charged words
Emitted streaks of lightning
So was the state
When mind wandered in every direction
Breaking through concrete structures.
What a distress it is
To a soulless body!
Will it glean pearls while returning?
Or
Hang its head in exhaustion?
Well,
If it turns up with pearls... fine.
For, it clothes clouds in a fine Raga
And conjures them up to rain
That she might sign off
Boats of pleasure with dreams
Only when it comes home drained out
That life convulses for breath
Whose autobiography it listens way back home!
What wakes of old-age it walks down its journey!
Which 'tear-dried' childish cheek it caresses along!
Long after

Translated from Telugu ● *NS Murty*   **319**

Earth and Heaven
Air, Water and Fire
Come together to distract
Does it care to look at me
Afresh...as if it has all begun anew?

◆

Gujjalam*

Daddy!
Shall I tell you a story?
Once there was a king
He had three daughters
And a son elder to them
They had a crow for friend
Then, they get hungry
There you are, laughing!
No! I won't tell you anymore.

You never stay put at home.
It would be nice if you do
Please daddy!
I promise I won't play in water
Complete homework properly
What is there
In all these books daddy?
All ABCDs?

Are you angry?
I am sorry.
Mommy, why this man gets angry
For nothing?

(Addressing his sister)
Why do you pout?
What happened to you, Pachi?

Make no mischief!
No playing pranks either!

Why? Doesn't that blood-sucker
Have parents, daddy?
It appears always alone on the tree.

Shall we play Kabaddi daddy?
Otherwise, hide and seek?
No hiding in bathrooms
Or bed rooms!

Take this book.
You like it, isn't it?
I love my mommy
I love you too, daddy!

Why should I go to school
Always by bus?
Why don't you send me by airplane?

Tomorrow is my birthday
If you don't bring me gift
I would mash you to chutney.

I will give you a chocolate
Go, and make merry.
And write your poems.

> * *Gujjalam- in childy jargon stands for Gulab Jamun,*
> *a noted south-Indian sweet delicacy.*

◆

BOLLOJU BABA

Apartheid

"Teacher! Can I give the bouquet to the Chief Guest?"
"No. You can't. We have already selected someone else."
And soon she realized the difference between
Her and that 'someone else': her tan.
Emptying tears and blood into the gorges of history
It plays chiaroscuro on the path of life.
She wanted to cry hoarse
That soul is superior to the shuck.
With reddened eyes and swollen face
She silently departed
Collecting all her prizes.

Ten years later...

Nobody understood why
The Chief Guest
After finishing her speech
Walked down to a student
With reddened eyes and swollen face
Placed the bouquet in her hand
And patted her on shoulder before leaving.

They will never understand for another ten years to come.

Translated from Telugu ● *NS Murty*

NISHIGANDHA

This Night

Effacing the last trace of cloudlets
Darkness thickens.
Whether to trade some pleasantries
Or to run after the dreams adrift
The jasmines of the sky blossom one after the other.

Deftly sieging the cheery butterflies of
Swoons within the bangled-hands
I must gently acquaint them soundlessness.

I long to live this night
Forgetting for a moment
The fragments of memories
The remotest dreams
And the toils of the day

Instead of delving deep within
I must course away from myself...
Sundering and scattering
The immutable gravity of fears
I must waft lighter and lighter...

As the chalky design in the foreyard,
Lying snug through the whole day,
Start pandiculating
For the occasional whiff of breeze
I must initiate my abc once more
With the corals spread across the yard.

Unveiling the blinds of heartaches
I must kiss him
For at least five minutes...
I must introduce this gentle night!

Under the breezing skies
The wild flowers scissor the winds.
A hearty touch in the palm
And there it is...
The warmth left by the lamp just put out.

There is reassurance for the night!
Before a fistful of light wakes me up
I must live this night to heart's content.

◆

Acknowledgements

A sincere attempt has been made to collect information about the poets and locate all copyright holders. Unless otherwise noted, copyright to the original poems is held by the individual poets.

1. Abd Wahed (born July 24, 1966)
    1wahed@gmail.com / Ph.: 91-7396103556

2. Aduri Satyavathi Devi (1948-2008)
    ASR Murty, 50-52-2, Seetammadhara, Visakhapatnam - 530013
    Ph.: 91-9441940653

3. Afsar (born April 11)
    afsartelugu@gmail.com / Ph.: 1-897-800-4638

4. Anil Dani (born March 7, 1981)
    anildyani@gmail.com / Ph.: 91-9703336688

5. Anisetti Rajita (born April 14, 1958)
    3-12-60, Kumarpalli, Hanamakonda, 506001, Warrangal, TS
    Ph.: 91-9849482462.

6. Arudra (Bhagavatula Sadasiva Sankara Sastry)
    (August 31,1925 - June 4, 1998)

7. Bala Sudhakaramauli (born June 22, 1987)
    champaavathi@gmail.com / Ph.: 91-9676493680

8. Bhaskar Kondreddy (born March 19, 1973)treescienceclub@gmail.com /
    Ph.: 91-9490330841

9. Bhavani Phani (born September 16, 1977)
    vhssaketh@gmail.com

10. Bobby Nee (born January 6, 1985)
    kranthi.kavi@gmail.com

11. Bolloju Baba (born August 15, 1971)
   bollojubaba@gmail.com / Ph.: 91-9849320434

12. BVV Prasad (born November 21, 1966)
   prasadbvv1@gmail.com / Ph.: 91-9032075415

13. Chavali Bangaramma (1897-1970)

14. Chintam Praveen (born November 10, 1981)
   drpraveen.kuc@gmailcom / Ph.: 91-9346886143

15. Devipriya (born August 5, 1951)
   https://te.wikipedia.org/wiki/<ûMç|¾jáT / Ph.: 91-9866111874

16. Duvvuri Rami Reddy (November 9, 1895 - 1947)

17. Elanaaga (born April 28, 1953)
   elanaaga@gmail.com / Ph.: 91-9866945424

18. Godavari Sarma (August 17, 1954 - February 8, 1990)
   syamalak13@gmail.com

19. HRK (born October 10, 1951)
   hrkkodidela@gmail.com / Ph.: 1-609-737-1457

20. Ismail (July 1, 1928 - November 25, 2003)

21. Jashua (September 28, 1895 - July 24, 1971)

22. Jayashree Naidu (born August 29, 1976)
   jayasmurli@gmail.com / Ph.: 91-9030012030

23. K. Geetha (born December 11, 1970)
   kgeetamadhavi@gmail.com / Ph.: 776-099-1795

24. Kalekuri Prasad (October 15, 1964 - May 17, 2013)

25. Kasula Linga Reddy (born January 12, 1966)drklraddy1966@gmail.com /
   Phs.: 91-9948900691; 91-8897811844

26. Katta Srinivas (born January 1, 1974)
   nivas.katta74@gmail.com / Ph.: 91-9885133969

27. Kavi Yakoob (born March 2, 1962)
   kaviyakoob62@gmail.com / Ph.: 91-9849156588

28. Kiran Gali (born October 8)
   kiran@galipar.com / Ph.: 91-9618537678

29. Koduri Vijay Kumar (born July 1, 1969)
   kodurivijay@gmail.com

30. Kondamudi Saikiran Kumar (born January 8, 1968)kskk@rediffmail.com
     / Ph.: 91-9702911151

31. Kopparthy Venkata Ramana Murthy (born January 9, 1959)
     kopparthyvrm@gmail.com / Ph.: 91-9849525765

32. Krishna Sastry (November 1, 1897 - February 24, 1980)

33. Kumara Varma K (born August 22, 1965)
     kcubev@rediffmail.com / Ph.: 91-9493436277

34. Madhuravani (born June 30)
     sumadhuravaani@gmail.com / Ph.: 49-17620934032 (Germany)

35. Mahesh Kumar Kathi (born December 12, 1976)
     Mahesh.kathi@gmail.com / Ph.: 91-9000998503

36. Manasa Chamarti (born March 23, 1984)manasa.chamarthi@gmail.com /
     Ph.: 91-9731899700

37. Maruvam Usha (born March 4)
     ushaa.raani@gmail.com

38. Mercy Margaret (born August 23, 1983)
     mercydachiever@gmail.com / Ph.: 91-9052809952

39. Mohan Rushi (born September 12)
     mohanrishi.73@gmail.com / Ph.: 91-8341725452

40. Mohanatulasi Ramineni (born December 11) tulasimohan11@gmail.com

41. Mukunda Rama Rao, Yellapu
     ymramarao@gmail.com / Ph.: 91-9908347273

42. Naleswaram Sankaram (born April 10, 1955)
     16-11-774/ 1, Sarada Apartments, Moosarambagh , Hyderabad-500 036
     Ph.: 91-9440451960

43. Nanda Kishore (born February 19, 1989)1234nandakishore@gmail.com /
     Phs.: 91-8712829212; 91-9515881085

44. Narayana Sarma Mallavajjala (born October 24, 1971)
     mana.sharma66@gmail.com / Ph.: 91-9177260385

45. Narayana SwamyVenkatayogi (born December 8, 1965)
     swamyv@gmail.com /

46. Nirmala Ghantasala (born August 5, 1957)nirmalaghantasala@gmail.com

47. Nirmala Kondepudi (born March 26, 1958)
     nirmalakondepudi@gmail.com

48. Nishigandha (born January 20)
     ykiran97@gmail.com

49. Prasuna Ravindran (born June 21, 1981)
     aprasuna@gmail.com / Ph.: 91-9703334053

50. PraveenaKolli (born May 15)
     praveena.kolli@gmail.com

51. Pulipati Guruswamy (born March 31, 1969)
     anandudu@gmail.com / Ph.: 91-98488879C4

52. Radhika Rimmalapudi (born June 20, 1983)
     RRK2K3@gmail.com

53. Raghavareddy Ramireddy (born June 1, 1974)
     ramireddyraghava@gmail.com / Ph.: 91-9652902192

54. Ravi Verelly (born June 16, 1968)
     ravinder.verelly@gmail.com / Ph.: 1-540-204-0556

55. Saif Ali Gore Syed (born January 1, 1978) directorsaifalisyed@gmai.com

56. Satishchandar (born October 29, 1958)
     http://www.satishchandar.com / Ph.: 91-9866192685

57. Shajahana (born June 14, 1974)
     shajahana74@gmail.com / Ph.: 91-7799059494

58. Siddhartha (born September 19, 1961)
     Kavisiddhartha@gmail.com / Ph.: 91-9603318460

59. Sikhamani (born October 30, 1957)
     kavisikhamani1956@gmail.com / Ph.: 91-9848202526

60. Silalolita (born July 12)
     kavishilalolitha@gmail.com / Ph.: 91-9391338676

61. Sivareddy, K (born August 6, 1943)
     H.No.16-2-740/75/40,VK Dhage Nazar, Gaddiannaram, Hyderabad-60
     Ph.: 040-24110547

62. Skybaaba (born March 2, 1972)
     skybaaba@gmail.com / Ph.: 91-9985420027

63. Sobha Raju (born April 5, 1978)
     shobharaju.b@gmail.com /91-9553129041

64. Sowbhagya (born November 25, 1954) palellavijayakumar@gmail.com /
     Ph.: 91-9848157909

65. Srinivas Vasudev (born July 3)
    vasudevadari@gmail.com

66. Sri Sri (April 30, 1910 - June 15, 1983)

67. Swarajyam Ramakrishna (August 15, 1947 - January 7, 1967)
    3, China Waltair Main Road, opp: e-seva, Vizag - 530017
    Ph.: 91-9347211537

68. Swati Kumari (born September 11, 1983)
    swathikumari@gmail.com

69. Tilak (August 21, 1921 - July 1,1966)

70. Trishna (born September 4)
    http://trishnaventa.blogspot.com

71. Tummala Deva Rao (born June 1, 1971)
    drdevaraonirmal@gmail.com / Ph.: 91-8985742274

72. Vadrevu Chinaveerabhadrudu (born March 28, 1962)
    chinaveera@gmail.com / Ph.: 91-9490957129

73. Vamsidhar Reddy (born September 28, 1986)
    secretwindow.vamc@gmail.com / Ph.: 91-9985958810

74. Vanaja Tatineni (born March 1)
    vanajavanamali@gmail.com / Ph.: 91-9985981666

75. Vazir Rehman (October 11, 1934 - April 28, 1983)

76. Vedula Satyanarayana Sastry (March 22, 1900 - 1976)

77. Vidyasagar P (born October 10, 1963)
    Ph.: 91-9963570174

78. Vimala (born May 1)
    vimalamorthala@gmail.com / Ph.: 98852 01686

79. Vinnakota Ravisankar (born March 5, 1964)
    rvinnako@yahoo.com / Ph.: 1-803-361-0335

80. Viswanatha Satyanarayana (September 10,1895 - October 18, 1976)

81. Yendluri Sudhakar (born January 21, 1959)
    sudhakaryendluri@gmail.com / Phs.: 91-9246650771; 91-8832419322

◆

AUTHOR INDEX

NS Murty (Born on 4th March 1950) is a bilingual poet and translator. A postgraduate in Applied Mathematics (1972) and MA English literature (1984) from Andhra University, he was also a graduate student in English at University of Houston, Texas during Spring 2011. He worked in National Sample Survey Organization under Ministry of Statistics and Programme Implementation, GOI, for 31 years before moving to GMR Group in 2006.

With his maternal uncle R S Krishna Moorthy (1939-2001), a short story writer, he embarked upon a project of translating 100 best short stories from Telugu to English. The Palette (1997) was published by Jyeshtha Literary Trust and The Easel (2015) was self-published. The Canvas and The Painting are in the offing. They together won the prestigious Katha-British Council South Asian Translation Award 2000 for the translation of Late Allam Seshagiri Rao's short story "Mrigatrishna".

Commemorating the 200 years of publication of "Lyrical Ballads" by Wordsworth and ST Coleridge, in 1996, poet Sowbhagya and Mr. Murty published "nuvvu-nEnU, gAnamU-gaLamu" a collection of their Telugu poetry.

Mr. RS Krishna Moorthy, on the occasion of his Shashtipooti in 1999, published NS Murty's collection of English poems "Incidental Muses". His second collection of poems "The Pen Chants" is on the anvil.

In 2013, EMESCO published "ivanDii mana vALLa ATalu", a Telugu translation of Dr. V. Raghunathan's very famous book "Games Indians Play" rendered from English by Sri SVM Sastry and Mr. Murty.

Mr. Murty's playlets for AIR Visakhapatnam "aham brahmAsmi" (2000) which is based on Human Genome Project and "jeeva nADi" (2002) on the life of Gandhiji were broadcast many times. His Translation "rasanAdam" (2004) won Akash Vani National Award.

He rendered over 1650 of world's best poems, short stories and essays into Telugu, and vice versa, in his blog "anuvAdalahari" (teluguanuvaadaalu.wordpress.com.). He can be reached on +91 7760991795 or through nsmurty4350@gmail.com.

Some of NS Murty's Works

"A Collection of Telugu Short Stories Rendered into English"

EMESCO

The Easel

RS Krishna Moorthy
N S Murty

INCIDENTAL MUSES

N.S. MURTY

The Palette

TRANSLATED TELUGU STORIES
R.S. Krishna Moorthy
N.S. Murty

* 9 7 8 0 9 9 7 7 3 6 3 0 4 *